Your Future

Your Future

by
George Sweeting

MOODY PRESS
CHICAGO

Other books by George Sweeting

Dedicated with appreciation to that select group of men
who out of love for Jesus Christ serve as trustees
of the Moody Bible Institute of Chicago:

I thank Phil Johnson for his guidance and expertise.

All Scripture quotations, except where noted otherwise, are from the King James Version.

Library of Congress Cataloging in Publication Data

Sweeting, George, 1924-
  Your future.

  1. Bible—Prophecies. 2. Eschatology. I. Title.
BS647.2.S94 1984   236   84-19049
ISBN: 0-8024-0404-9 (pbk.)

1 2 3 4 5 6 7 Printing BC Year 88 87 86 85 84

Printed in the United States of America

Contents

Introduction

Why Study Prophecy?

Ignorance of God's prophetic outline, failure to know God's program for the Church, the nations, and Israel, is the cause of the overwhelming amount of error and misunderstanding of the events of the future.

—M. R. DeHaan

"The bloom of beauty on Apostolic Christianity was created by the upward look," theologian James Denney once said.

Dr. Denney was right. History shows that the church has been healthiest when the saints have most eagerly awaited the return of the Savior. Our Lord Himself encouraged watchfulness with a series of parables in Matthew 24-25.

Expectation breeds commitment. No one is a more devoted disciple than the one who is ready for his Lord to appear at any moment. And the normal fruit of the legitimate study of prophecy is a deeper consecration that grows out of that earnest hope.

That must be clearly understood at the outset, for although in recent years prophecy has been a popular theme of books and Bible studies, the proper perspective has largely been lost. Biblical prophecy has been studied out of mere curiosity, taught with detached pedantry, and preached for its sensational impact.

Foolish speculation has repeatedly proved to be wrong, and yet misguided individuals still persist in trying to determine dates, predict events, and find significance in every headline. Others use their prophetic views as a club, assaulting everyone they encounter with their particular view and scorning those who see things differently. Still others, perhaps reacting to the fanaticism of some, shelve the study of prophecy completely, ignoring all biblical teaching about Christ's return. Theological schools, not wishing to be controversial, often avoid any study of prophecy whatever. Confused by the diverse views, they opt to neglect the subject rather than face the difficult task of sorting out truth from error.

All of those approaches have done more harm than good, and I sense an urgent need for the church to return to a biblical approach in the study of our Lord's return. Wilbur M. Smith said, "The study of the prophetic Scripture is more important today . . . than at any time . . . since the Reformation, if not since the days of the apostles."[1] He made that statement more than twenty years ago, but it is even more true today.

Here are three points to remember throughout this study of biblical prophecy:

- *The Scriptures Are Full of Prophecy*

First, prophecy is not incidental to divine revelation. More than a fourth of the Bible is predictive prophecy. Approximately one-third of it has yet to be fulfilled. Both the Old and New Testaments are full of promises about the return of Jesus Christ. Over 1,800 references appear in the Old Testament, and seventeen Old Testament books give prominence to this theme. Of the 260 chapters in the New Testament, there are more than 300 references to the Lord's return—one out of every thirty verses. Twenty-three of the twenty-seven New Testament books refer to this great event. Three of the four other books are single-chapter letters written to individuals concerning a particular subject, and the fourth is Galatians, which does imply Christ's coming again. For every prophecy on the first coming of Christ, there are

1. Wilbur M. Smith, *World Crisis and the Prophetic Scriptures* (Chicago: Moody, 1950), p. 14.

eight on Christ's second coming.

Paul wrote to Timothy, "All scripture is given by inspiration of God, and is profitable for doctrine, for reproof, for correction, for instruction in righteousness: That the man [or woman] of God may be perfect, thoroughly furnished unto all good works" (2 Timothy 3:16-17). If we are to know the Word of God as He would have us know it, we must study prophecy.*

Our Lord Himself referred to the prophetic Scriptures time and again. He lived in the awareness of prophecy, for fulfillment of prophecy was all around Him. Let me illustrate from Matthew's gospel.

Matthew, writing to a primarily Jewish readership, emphasized that the life of Christ consistently intersected with Old Testament prophecies. For example, in chapter 1, Matthew tells that Jesus was born of a virgin. In verse 22, he writes, "Now all this was done, that it might be fulfilled which was spoken of the Lord by the prophet." Repeatedly, he emphasizes that certain events in the life of Christ took place in fulfillment of prophecies, "that it might be fulfilled which was spoken of the Lord by the prophet" (v. 22; cf. v. 23). His life was planned and foretold by God, including His death.

In Acts 10, Peter's message to the Jews was "To him [Jesus] give all the prophets witness, that through his name whosoever believeth in him shall receive remission of sins" (v. 43). His birth was prophesied, His life was prophesied, His death was prophesied, the period of time He spent in the grave was prophesied, His resurrection was prophesied, and His second advent was prophesied. All prophecy in one way or another points to Him.

Jesus Himself emphasized the truth of His second coming. He announced it, He repeated it, He expounded on it, and He reemphasized it. And just to make certain we do not miss it, the Scriptures end with "Surely I come quickly. Amen. Even so, come, Lord Jesus" (Revelation 22:20).

---

*The word *prophecy* can have two meanings. It can be simply *forth-telling*, or speaking forth revealed truth, as the Old Testament prophets did when they delivered messages from God that were not necessarily predictive. Or it can be *foretelling*—predicting the future. Throughout this book, when I use the term *prophecy*, unless noted otherwise, I am speaking of *foretelling*, or predictive prophecy.

• *Prophecy Is Full of Hope*

It has been said that man can live about forty days without food, about three days without water, and about eight
minutes without air—but only one second without HOPE.

A second point to keep in mind in the study of prophecy is
that prophecy is full of hope. The prophetic message of
Scripture is not primarily a message of doom. The second
coming of Jesus Christ is referred to as "that blessed hope"
(Titus 2:13). For believers, the whole of prophetic revelation
is a source of great hope.

Bible prophecy answers questions that nothing else will
answer. Where else could we learn about life after death?
The future of the earth? The promise of resurrection? The
believer's rewards?

For the believer, the return of Jesus Christ holds the
promise of eternal existence with Him, unbroken fellowship with all of heaven, and the end of tears, sorrow, sickness, and death. The apostle John wrote, "We know that,
when he shall appear, we shall be like him; for we shall see
him as he is" (1 John 3:2). Such an existence is the hope of
every believer.

Dr. Reuben A. Torrey, second president of the Moody Bible Institute, stated: "The latter truth [the second coming of
Christ] transformed *my whole idea of life;* it broke the *power of the world and its ambition over me,* and filled my life
with *the most radiant optimism* even under the most discouraging circumstances" (italics added).[2] Dr. Torrey was
asked, "Is not the doctrine of Christ's personal and near
coming one of practical power and helpfulness?" He replied, "It is transforming the lives of more men and women
than almost any doctrine I know of."[3]

Dr. James M. Gray explained how this truth worked in his
life:

> There are at least *five things which this hope effected in my
> life . . . it awakened a real love and enthusiasm for the study of
> every part of God's Word;* it quickened my zeal in Christian

2. William Culbertson, *Christ the Hope of the World!* (address given at
   WMBI Second Coming Conference, May 1954), p. 11.
3. Reuben A. Torrey, "He Is Coming," *Gospel Herald,* 1 September 1962,
   p. 17.

service, especially in foreign missions; it delivered my mind from an *over-weening ambition for worldly success and the praise of man;* it developed patience and quietness in the face of unjust treatment; and *it broke the bands of covetousness* and set me free to give of my substance to the Lord. (Italics added)[4]

There are those who teach that believers should not look forward to the coming of Jesus Christ to take them away. Believers will not be taken away, they say, before the Lord pours out His wrath on this unbelieving world. They believe that Christians will go through the time now known as the Great Tribulation (Matthew 24:21).

But I am convinced that is not the message of Scripture. We are told to look for our Lord's return—not God's judgment. Paul wrote to the Thessalonians with this message of hope: "God hath not appointed us to wrath, but to obtain salvation by our Lord Jesus Christ" (1 Thessalonians 5:9). It is a message of hope without fear.

- *Hope Is Full of Faith*

Finally, remember that biblical hope is confident, patient expectation. The word *hope* in Scripture is a term of certainty. To say that we hope for the return of the Lord is not to say that we are uncertain about His coming. His coming for His own is certain.

The Greek word translated "hope" in the New Testament is *elpizō*, which means "to anticipate with confident expectation." *Elpizō* is also translated "trust" in several New Testament verses. Hope is one of the three evidences of salvation—faith, hope, and love—referred to by the apostle Paul throughout the epistles (see 1 Corinthians 13:13; Colossians 1:4-5; 1 Thessalonians 1:3).

In Romans 8:23-25, Paul wrote, "We . . . groan within ourselves, waiting eagerly for our adoption as sons, the redemption of our body. For in hope we have been saved, but hope that is seen is not hope; for why does one also hope for what he sees? But if we hope for what we do not see, with perseverance we wait eagerly for it" (NASB*).

*New American Standard Bible.
4. Culbertson, *Christ the Hope of the World!*, p. 11.

In other words, ours is a confident hope that produces a patient anticipation. In 1 Corinthians 15, anticipating that time "when this corruptible shall have put on incorruption . . . [and] Death is swallowed up in victory" (v. 54), Paul writes, "Therefore, my beloved brethren, be ye stedfast, unmoveable, always abounding in the work of the Lord, forasmuch as ye know that your labour is not in vain in the Lord" (v. 58).

Cynics mock. Do-gooders tell us the world is moving upward and onward. But the believer in Jesus Christ possesses abundant faith even in a dying world. 1 Peter 1:13 urges us, "Therefore, gird your minds for action, keep sober in spirit, fix your *hope* completely on the grace to be brought to you at the revelation of Jesus Christ" (NASB, italics added).

That is the perspective of one who knows Jesus is coming. It is the patience that grows out of the blessed hope of His return. This is our purpose in studying Bible prophecy.

Pastor Horatius Bonar lived in the glow of Christ's coming. As he would conclude his day's ministry, he would draw the curtains of his window and utter as he looked upward, "Perhaps tonight, Lord!" In the morning, as he awoke and looked out on the dawn of a new day, he would pray, looking up into the sky, "Perhaps today, Lord!"

1

Return

Jesus Is Coming

The Christian believer of our day cannot but be aware of the fact that he is living in an eschatological age, in which the thinking of all men—statesmen, historians, scientists, educators, theologians—is agitated by the possibility of the rapid consummation of history.

—William F. Kerr

One thing is clear from Bible prophecy: Jesus is coming. Not everyone agrees, of course, on the proper interpretation of scriptural teaching on the subject of Jesus' return to earth, but Bible students are virtually unanimous that Scripture teaches He *will* return. Every book of the New Testament makes reference to the second coming. Christians have always looked for Jesus Christ to return. The early church lived in the glow of that hope; they were confident that He might return at any moment.

But despite the unanimity about the question of *whether* Jesus will return, there is a great deal of disagreement in eschatology—the study of future things—concerning the particulars. The questions of when and how He will return have always caused spirited disagreement. At the outset of this study, it is important that we put those issues in perspective.

The first basic area of conflict in eschatology involves the Millennium, the thousand-year period spoken of in Revelation 20:2-7 during which Christ rules over His kingdom. Three major views are prevalent: amillennialism, postmillennialism, and premillennialism.

Amillennialists say that there will not be a literal Millennium here on earth. They believe the millennial manifestation of the kingdom of God is spiritual, not literal, and that Christ's return will mark the end of the ages and the beginning of eternity. Thus they teach that we are in the Millennium now. Amillennialists would plot the events of the present age like this:

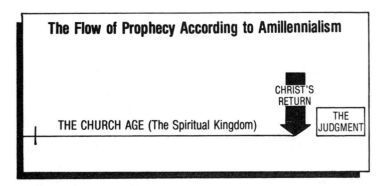

The Flow of Prophecy According to Amillennialism

CHRIST'S RETURN

THE CHURCH AGE (The Spiritual Kingdom)

THE JUDGMENT

Some amillennial theorists would vary that pattern slightly, but all would agree that there will not be a literal, earthly age known as the Millennium during which Christ would reign in His physical presence here on earth.

Postmillennialists have all but disappeared from contemporary theology, but new variations of postmillennial eschatology keep emerging. Postmillennialism was popular in the eighteenth and nineteenth centuries, when it was commonly thought that things were getting better and the world was improving. Postmillennialists believed that the millennial kingdom would be ushered in through the preaching of the gospel, as Christianity spread and the church gained influence. Here is how classic postmillennialists viewed future events:

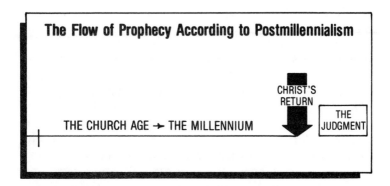

The Flow of Prophecy According to Postmillennialism

CHRIST'S RETURN

THE CHURCH AGE → THE MILLENNIUM   THE JUDGMENT

According to postmillennialism, the church, not Christ, is responsible for bringing about the Kingdom age, and Christ will not return until after the completion of that age—hence the name *post*millennialism.

Premillennialists interpret biblical prophecy more literally. They believe in an actual age of one thousand years when Jesus Christ will be present physically on earth to reign over all kingdoms. This is a chart of a typical premillennial interpretation of the flow of prophetic events:

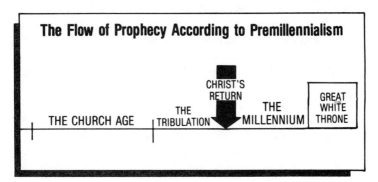

The Flow of Prophecy According to Premillennialism

CHRIST'S RETURN

THE CHURCH AGE   THE TRIBULATION   THE MILLENNIUM   GREAT WHITE THRONE

How do sincere Bible students who are all seeking the truth arrive at fundamentally different conclusions about such a key area of biblical teaching? The answer is found in the hermeneutical method—the system of interpretation—of each view. Of the three major millennial views, only premillennialism can be supported by normal methods of biblical interpretation.

Both amillennialism and postmillennialism rely heavily on allegorical methods of interpretation. Premillennialism, however, interprets prophecy literally when possible, acknowledging symbolic meaning only when it is obvious. The rule premillennialists employ is: When the plain sense of Scripture makes good sense, seek no other sense.

The perspective of this book is premillennial. Without going into the many arguments given to support or to refute each view, let me simply affirm that I believe consistent hermeneutics demands a premillennial eschatology. Having studied Bible prophecy for many years, I cannot get away from the fact that the clearest, most direct teaching in the New Testament indicates that Jesus will return personally to set up His kingdom on earth.

THE RAPTURE QUESTION

The second fundamental area of disagreement concerns the rapture, the taking away of the saints from the earth. Most of the disagreement on this issue exists between premillennialists, as they are the only ones who see the rapture as an event separate from the second coming of Christ.

Premillennial eschatology maintains that the return of Jesus Christ occurs in two stages. At the rapture, the Lord comes *for* the saints, and they rise to meet Him in the air (1 Thessalonians 4:17). At that time, His feet do not actually touch the earth. His coming to earth *with* the saints is stage two.

Most premillennialists agree that the rapture will occur, but they do not always agree about its meaning or about where it fits within the prophetic scheme.

The word *rapture* itself does not appear in Scripture, but it is the term theologians use for the event described in 1 Thessalonians 4:16-17:

> The Lord Himself will descend from heaven with a shout, with the voice of the archangel, and with the trumpet of God; and the dead in Christ shall rise first. Then we who are alive and remain shall be caught up together with them in the clouds to meet the Lord in the air, and thus we shall always be with the Lord. (NASB)

First Corinthians 15:51-52 says, "Behold, I tell you a mystery; we shall not all sleep, but we shall all be changed, in a moment, in the twinkling of an eye, at the last trumpet; for the trumpet will sound, and the dead will be raised imperishable, and we shall be changed" (NASB). The question is, When will that happen? How does it fit into the scheme of future events, and specifically, when will it occur with respect to the Tribulation?

The Tribulation will be a time characterized by incredible calamity, including wars, earthquakes, disasters, heresy, and global misery (Matthew 24:6-13). Many students of prophecy connect the Tribulation with the seventieth week spoken of by Daniel in Daniel 9:27.

Those who subscribe to the view of a posttribulational rapture believe the rapture will occur subsequent to the Tribulation. They believe that the church, all the redeemed of this age, will remain on earth during the Tribulation. Thus they view the Tribulation as a time of purging for the church, as well as a time of judgment for the world.

The midtribulational view, not widely embraced, places the rapture in the middle of the Tribulation. According to this view, the church will be taken out in the middle of Daniel's seventieth week, before the worst judgments are sent.

The pretribulational position, which I believe most accurately reflects biblical teaching, holds that believers of this age will miss the Tribulation completely. Of the three groups, only pretribulationists believe that the Lord Jesus could return at any moment. Both posttribulationists and midtribulationists are looking for the beginning of the Tribulation. Pretribulationists look for the coming of Jesus Christ in the rapture.

Again, it is not my purpose in this brief chapter to give all the arguments for and against each view. The reason for my commitment to the premillennial, pretribulational viewpoint can be summarized as this: Of all the major eschatological systems, pretribulational premillennialism best answers the many questions that arise in the study of Bible prophecy; it holds to a consistent, normal method of Bible interpretation; and it emphasizes the importance of watchfulness and readiness in light of the imminence of Jesus' return.

Having said that, let me emphasize that there is room for diverse points of view in the fellowship of Christ's body. I value close friendships with brothers and sisters in Christ

who do not share my views in the area of eschatology. A
person's interpretation of prophecy should never be the sole
test for choosing those with whom he will fellowship.

Some points of Bible prophecy, however, are not open to
discussion. Where the Bible speaks clearly, we must believe
it implicitly. And much about the return of Jesus Christ is
clear and non-debatable. True believers are in complete
agreement on these issues.

Jesus is coming. We began this chapter by asserting that
Jesus Christ will come again to earth. His coming is the
focal point of all biblical prophecy and the greatest certainty of all the things we look for as believers. Some 1,800
references in the Old Testament prophesy the advent of a
victorious, reigning Messiah. They are yet to be fulfilled.
And all of the New Testament calls us to watchfulness in the
expectation that He will return for us.

"If I go and prepare a place for you," He promised, "I will
come again, and receive you to Myself; that where I am,
there you may be also" (John 14:3, NASB).

Jesus is coming personally. Jesus' return will be real and
personal. As the disciples stood gazing into heaven after the
Lord's ascension, two angels appeared to them and said,
"Men of Galilee, why do you stand looking into the sky? *This
Jesus,* who has been taken up from you into heaven, *will
come in just the same way* as you have watched Him go into
heaven" (Acts 1:11, NASB, italics added). The second coming of Jesus Christ is not spiritual or symbolic. He will
come physically, in person, the same way that He left.

Jesus is coming visibly. Revelation 1:7 declares, "Behold,
He is coming with the clouds, and every eye will see Him,
even those who pierced Him" (NASB). Jesus said, "Just as
the lightning comes from the east, and flashes even to the
west, so shall the coming of the Son of Man be" (Matthew
24:27, NASB). He went on to reveal, "The sign of the Son of
Man will appear in the sky, and then all the tribes of the
earth will mourn, and they will see the Son of Man coming
on the clouds of the sky with power and great glory" (v. 30,
NASB).

Jesus is coming victoriously. Finally, Jesus' return to earth will mark His ultimate victory over all the forces of evil and unbelief in the world. Second Thessalonians 2 describes the Antichrist, the "lawless one . . . whom the Lord will slay with the breath of His mouth and bring to an end by the appearance of His coming" (v. 8, NASB). Every passage that speaks of the return of Christ describes a great victory consummated by His appearing. Actually, Armageddon will not be a battle at all. There will be no prolonged struggle, no real resistance, and no hand-to-hand combat between the Lord and those who oppose Him. When He appears, the battle will be won instantly.

Jesus is coming suddenly. In Matthew 24:44, Jesus said, "The Son of Man is coming at an hour when you do not think He will" (NASB). Most people will be caught by surprise when the Lord returns. I am afraid most Christians do not really live in the expectation of His coming. Be careful—for when you begin to forget He is coming, and when you begin to despair that He really will return, that is the time He is most likely to appear.

"I am coming quickly," He says (Revelation 22:20). Happy is the heart that can echo, "Amen. Come, Lord Jesus."

2

Revelation

An Outline of God's Calendar

Believing as we do that there is no hope for this floundering, blundering old world in this atomic age through the efforts of man, we turn to the Word of God for an answer, and find that God has a program, and a plan which is running exactly on time.

—M. R. DeHaan

Perhaps the best known and least understood book of all prophetic literature is the book of Revelation, which is also called the Apocalypse. Revelation holds the key to all biblical prophecy. In fact, an outline of Revelation is an outline of the course of prophecy. Correctly understood, this final book of Scripture makes clear God's plan for the last days.

Written around A.D. 100, the book of Revelation is as relevant today as it was in the first and second centuries. It speaks of politics, power struggles, disasters, and worldwide turmoil—in many ways, it seems more fitting for today than for the time in which it was written. One can hardly look at the newspaper and compare it to Revelation without experiencing a strong feeling that the things prophesied long ago may come to pass very soon.

John, the beloved apostle of Jesus Christ, is the human author of the book of Revelation. In it he records and de-

scribes a vision revealed to him while he was exiled on the
Isle of Patmos. The vision he unfolds shows graphically the
outline of God's plan for the ages and the consummation of
world history.

Revelation may at first seem to be one of the most confus-
ing books in all of Scripture, for it speaks of future things,
often in symbolic language. But we must understand that
God did not give it to us to confuse us. The first word in the
Greek text of Revelation is *apokalupsis*, the Greek word for
"disclosure," from which we get the title *Revelation*. Thus,
Revelation is a disclosure, an unfolding, meant to enlighten
us rather than confuse us. And verse 3 of chapter 1 gives
this encouragement to those who would study its truths:
"Blessed is he that readeth, and they that hear the words of
this prophecy, and keep those things which are written
therein: for the time is at hand."

Clearly, Revelation was meant to be an aid to understanding God's plan for the end times and the return of Jesus
Christ. We can only benefit from studying it.

THE KEY TO THE BOOK OF REVELATION

In Revelation, one verse more than any other gives us the
key to understanding the book as a whole. That verse is
Revelation 1:19: "Write the things which thou hast seen, and
the things which are, and the things which shall be hereafter." In that verse the resurrected and glorified Lord Jesus
instructs the aged apostle to write in three tenses—past,

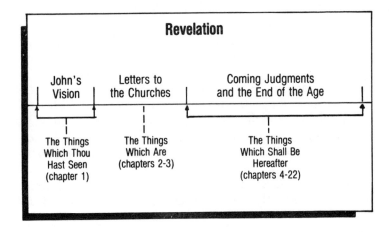

present, and future. Looking carefully at the book of Revelation as a whole, we find that it breaks down exactly into that pattern (see chart).

In chapter 1, John gives us background information about a vision he had of the Lord Jesus, essentially in the past tense. In chapters 2 and 3, he records a series of messages to some of the churches in Asia Minor. Although those messages contain prophetic material—in fact, close examination shows that they are a kind of prophetic history of the church age—they are primarily letters to specific churches that existed in John's day, therefore written in the present tense.

The future tense chapters make up the bulk of the book of Revelation. From chapter 4 through the end, the apostle reveals details about the Tribulation, the second coming of Christ, the Millennium, the great white throne judgment, and the establishment of the new heavens and the new earth.

THE CONTENTS OF THE BOOK OF REVELATION

The following is an outline of several key prophetic events described in Revelation.

The church age. With the exception of Revelation 2-3, nothing in all the predictive prophecy of Scripture deals with events in the time between Christ's first and second advents—the period known as the church age. The Old Testament prophets had nothing at all to say about the church age; it is as if in looking across the ages they could see the mountaintops of Christ's first and second comings but not the valley of the church age between. New Testament writers in general carry through with that pattern for a very good reason: the next event on God's prophetic calendar is the return of Jesus Christ for His saints. If there were other prophecies to be fulfilled before He could come, we would not be looking for and eagerly awaiting His return. Consequently, predictive prophecy is silent about the church age.

Revelation 2-3, although not predicting events that will occur in the church age, has a great deal to say about the character of this age. Its prophecy comes in the form of letters from the Lord Jesus to some churches in Asia Minor.

He praises and rebukes the churches for their strengths and weaknesses, and He gives a unique message to each one.

These churches were local assemblies, but many Bible students view the messages to them as forming a chronological outline of church history. Others see the characteristics of the various churches as typical of different churches throughout the entire church age. Whichever view is accurate, it seems clear that the intent of the Lord's message to these churches goes far beyond the scope of the local assemblies as they existed in the apostle John's time. A summary of Jesus' message to each church reveals their applicability today.

Ephesus, the backslidden church (2:1-7). Jesus warned these believers that because they had left their first love, they were in need of revival. He told them to remember their former position, to repent of their sinful backsliding, and to retrace their wayward steps.

Smyrna, the persecuted church (2:8-11). Jesus encouraged this church in their tribulation and poverty, promising a crown of life to those who were faithful unto death.

Pergamum, the worldly church (2:12-17). Jesus commended the church in Pergamum for holding fast His name and for not denying the faith, but He rebuked them for holding the doctrines of Balaam and the Nicolaitans, which were doctrines of compromise with the world.

Thyatira, the idolatrous church (2:18-29). The Lord rebuked these believers for allowing a false teacher into their midst, a woman He called Jezebel, who was leading some of His servants into idolatry. He promised judgment for her and encouraged them to hold fast until His return.

Sardis, the dying church (3:1-6). Christ admonished believers in Sardis to repent and to hold fast to sound teaching, promising those who would heed His words that they would walk with Him in white if they remained undefiled.

Philadelphia, the healthy church (3:7-13). Jesus had nothing but commendation and encouraging words for this church, before whom He promised to set an open door that no man could shut.

Laodicea, the lukewarm church (3:14-22). Christ warned this smug and self-satisfied group that if they were not zealous in their repentance, He would spew them out of His mouth.

From that brief overview, it is easy to see that Jesus' messages to those few churches at the conclusion of the first century are timeless messages that cover the scope of the entire church age. They speak to churches today as powerfully as they spoke to the churches of the apostle's day.

The rapture. The rapture of the church is not specifically described in Revelation, but it is pictured in chapter 4 as the apostle John is translated into heaven with the words "Come up hither" (v. 1). This account of John being taken to heaven comes just after Jesus' letters to the churches and immediately before the judgments that begin in chapter 6. It parallels the rapture, which is to come at the end of the church age and prior to the Tribulation.

The Tribulation. Descriptions of the judgments that will take place on earth during the Tribulation fill up the majority of the book of Revelation. A seven-sealed scroll is introduced in chapter 5. As each seal is broken, a different judgment is poured out on the earth. The judgments include apostasy, war, famine, death, martyrdom, and anarchy. At the opening of the seventh seal, heaven is silent for about a half hour, and then seven trumpets are blown. With each trumpet comes a new judgment—the sea turns to blood, the sun becomes dark, stars fall, the earth's water is poisoned, and so on.

After the seven trumpets are blown, seven vials of judgment are poured out. Disease, pestilence, and calamity result as all the world hurtles headlong toward a final showdown between the forces of good and evil. During this time, the Antichrist and his false prophet deceive the entire world and set up an evil kingdom to rule over it. It is a terrifying time of martyrdom, fear, torment, judgment, natural disaster, and every woe the earth has ever seen. We will study this time in detail in chapter 6.

The Battle of Armageddon. Revelation 19 describes the climactic battle between Satan's army and the Lord Jesus. Christ destroys all the forces of hell with the sword coming out of His mouth, symbolic of the Word of God. The culmination of this great battle comes when the Antichrist and his false prophet are cast into the lake of fire.

The return of Jesus Christ. The second coming of Christ coincides with the Battle of Armageddon. He appears in the clouds of heaven and instantly destroys the powers of evil.

The Millennium. Revelation 20 describes the thousand-year period during which Jesus Christ rules over the earth. During this time, Satan is bound in a bottomless abyss, unable to affect world events.

The great white throne judgment. Revelation 20:11-15 tells of this great and awesome judgment in which all who have rejected Christ are eternally consigned to the lake of fire.

The new heaven and new earth. The ultimate restoration of all things is described in the closing two chapters of Revelation. The whole earth and all of heaven are remade and united, and those who have yielded to Christ dwell with Him throughout eternity.

THE CHRONOLOGY OF THE BOOK OF REVELATION

Viewed as a whole, the book of Revelation presents a complete outline of premillennial, pretribulational prophecy. Notice that the order of events in Revelation exactly parallels the pretribulationists' view of the prophetic scheme (see chart on p. 29).

We cannot know when the rapture will take place and the Tribulation will begin, but it is significant to note that almost twenty centuries after these prophecies were written, their fulfillment looks more imminent than ever. Events in world politics, scientific advances, and the spiritual decline of society have all come together to make what once seemed like fanciful symbolism appear to be tomorrow's news.

Our Lord may yet tarry for a long while, but in the meantime we can be encouraged in knowing that things are right on schedule in the plan of God. All the turmoil and confusion in world events has deep meaning in light of God's purpose for the ages. God cannot be confounded. He is in control, no matter how much influence the powers of darkness may seem to have today. His plan is coming to fulfillment, just as He prophesied so long ago.

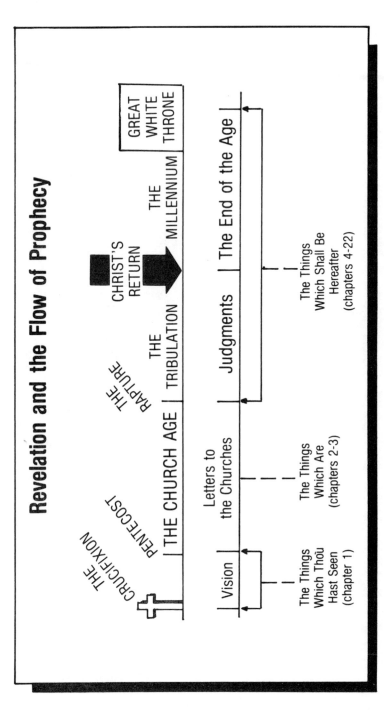

3

Readiness

A Warning Against Apostasy

The doctrine of the second coming has failed, so far as we are concerned, if it does not make us realize that at every moment of every year in our lives Donne's question, "What if this present were the world's last night?" is equally relevant.

—C. S. Lewis

The year was 1939, and the Spanish Civil War was almost over. Just outside Madrid, the rebel General Mola was ready to attack.

Someone asked which of his four columns of troops would be the first to enter the city. His answer has become world famous. "The fifth," he responded.

The general was saying that his most important column was a band of rebel sympathizers in the city. They were behind the Loyalist lines helping him already.

Since General Mola's remark, the term *fifth column* has been used worldwide. It is the description of a traitor, one who helps the enemy from within.

Not many years later during World War II, a fifth column in Norway brought about that country's collapse. Its leader, Vidkun Quisling, became the unhappy country's puppet premier. At the end of the war, Norway was freed, and Quisling was put to death for treason.

Betrayal is an ugly business, but it is very common in history. Down through the centuries even the church of Jesus Christ has had its Quislings. Some professing the Christian faith have attacked the authority of Scripture, denied basic Bible doctrine, and sown division, discouragement, and doubt. They have even challenged the foundational truth that salvation is by faith in Jesus Christ alone.

Opposition from within is clearly recognized in the Bible. The Bible even describes this by the specific word *apostasy*. Apostasy has left its tragic and sorry wake in every generation. The Bible tells us that it will run its course, then disappear forever under God's eternal judgment.

Let us take a look at apostasy—its nature, its course, and how to be ready to confront it.

THE NATURE OF APOSTASY

Apostasy is opposition to the Christian faith from those within. People who once professed the faith and still call themselves believers become its enemies.

The Greek word from which we derive the word *apostasy* means "a falling away, a rebellion or revolt." In New Testament times, to apostatize meant to desert a station or a post. The same word was used by the Greek biographer Plutarch to describe a political revolution.

In apostasy, professing Christians say to the church and to the world at large, "The things the Bible teaches aren't what they seem to be. This truth is not a truth. This fact is not a fact." And the attack comes not from enemies outside the faith, but from those who claim to be believers within.

The church was still in swaddling clothes when Peter described how bad things would become. In 2 Peter 2, he speaks of "false teachers" who would bring in "damnable heresies, even denying the Lord that bought them" (v. 1).

And it has been exactly that way. Apostasy has always brought deadly, all-out warfare. Apostasy discredits the Christian faith.

The source of apostasy is the mind and heart of Satan. Jesus revealed this fact in the parable of the tares in Matthew 13:24-30. He said the kingdom of heaven was like a farmer who sowed good seed in a field. But when the seed sprouted and grew, it came up full of weeds.

His servants were greatly troubled. "Didn't you plant good seed?" they asked.

"Yes," He said. "My seed was good. But an enemy has sown the weeds. Don't pull them now. Wait until the harvest. Then we'll gather the wheat and burn the weeds."

"The good seed are the children of the kingdom; but the tares are the children of the wicked one; the enemy that sowed them is the devil" (Matthew 13:38-39). Satan is the source of apostasy.

Apostates are the devil's agents, the fifth column inside the church. The New Testament book of Jude tells us in verse 4 that they have crept into the church by deceit.

Were they really true believers? John says they were not. His answer is found in 1 John 2. "They went out from us," he writes in verse 19, "but they were not of us." And then he adds, "If they had been of us [if they had been bona fide believers] they would no doubt have continued with us."

Oh, yes, there are pretenders in the church, and some are even secret agents. But God knows who they are. In 2 Timothy 2:19, Paul says, "Nevertheless the foundation of God standeth sure . . . The Lord knoweth them that are his. And, Let every one that nameth the name of Christ depart from iniquity."

Where are we right now in this deadly warfare? What is the history of the conflict, and what will be its outcome?

THE COURSE OF APOSTASY

In the church's early years, apostasy was already rearing its ugly head. In the year A.D. 85, the aged apostle John wrote, "Even now are there many antichrists" (1 John 2:18). The book of Jude was written because apostasy had already appeared. Other books such as Colossians were written because of this same need.

The Holy Spirit revealed to the writers of Scripture that apostasy would continue through the centuries. In 2 Thessalonians 2:3, Paul tells the church that Christ will not return to catch away His own until apostasy has reached its final climax. The great apostate will be the Antichrist. "Let no man deceive you by any means," the apostle writes, "for that day shall not come, except there come a falling away first [an apostasy], and that man of sin be revealed, the son of perdition."

What is the Bible saying? Simply that the tide of turning away will continue through the present age. It will reach its climax with the coming of the Antichrist. Then and only then will this age close as Christ catches up the church.

Gnosticism was one of the earliest errors within the church. Neoplatonism was another. Monarchianism soon came along to deny the Trinity.

It was apostasy in the church that set the stage for the Reformation. In due time came the so-called higher criticism which denied that the Bible had been written as the Bible teaches it was written. Men like Eichhorn, Graf, and Wellhausen attacked the authorship of Genesis and other books in the Pentateuch. Others tried to destroy the credibility of great books of prophecy.

In more recent years, the church has had to contend with liberalism and neo-orthodoxy. And not too many years ago, apostates even claimed that God was dead.

In our day, once great denominations have been overwhelmed. So-called Christian colleges and seminaries are infiltrated by professors who doubt, deny, or water down the Bible as the Word of God. Thousands of well-intentioned people have graduated from these schools and then set out to preach without the heart and truth of the gospel message. And Christians in the pews have been spiritually starved, misled, and blinded by unbelief and error.

In general, three kinds of error have been sown.

- The claim is made that the Bible is a human book, not the living Word of God.
- A substitute kind of faith is taught, which denies the power of Christ to change a person's life—"a form of godliness, but denying the power thereof" (2 Timothy 3:5).
- Distortions of the Christian faith are offered as substitutes. These are similar to the historic Christian faith, but in every case something is added, overemphasized, or left out. Thus, followers fall short of full dependence on Jesus Christ alone.

Like a mighty whirlwind, apostasy sweeps on, taking its
toll. Yet God is using even this to accomplish His great
purposes. Apostasy is winnowing out true believers from
unbelievers. Resistance to its wiles is strengthening true
Christians. And the fact of apostasy wakens believers to
vigilance and readiness.

HOW CAN WE COMBAT APOSTASY?

Apostasy is an issue of life or death—eternal life or eternal death. For a century it has been the privilege of the
Moody Bible Institute to place itself squarely across the
onward path of apostasy. We have taught and shared and
sown the historic gospel of Jesus Christ for one hundred
years. We have trained young men and women to teach and
preach the unchanging Word of God. The Bible itself has
been our primary and supreme textbook.

The Word of God declares that there is one body, one
Spirit, one Lord, one faith, and one baptism (Ephesians 4:4-
5). Apostasy claims to have a substitute way, but it leads to
destruction. There are, however, at least four things we can
do to combat apostasy.

- *Recognize it.* Many Christians neither see nor hear the
  signs of apostasy. An alarm should sound in our minds
  and hearts when we hear or read a message that says
  the Bible is not the inerrant Word of God. We should
  catch the slightest whisper that suggests there is a way
  to eternal life other than Jesus Christ.

  Almost always, false teaching claims to honor Christ.
  Many groups profess to "go by the Bible." We need to
  be like the Bereans, who "received the word with all
  readiness of mind, and searched the scriptures daily,
  whether those things were so" (Acts 17:11, italics added).
- *Resist wrong teaching.* If you find an error, do something. Raise a firm yet gracious question, and warn
  others if error does exist.

  Jude exhorts us to "contend for the faith which was
  once delivered unto the saints" (v. 3). Only that faith can
  save; anything less is not enough. We have a responsibil-

ity to see that the faith given to us is unaltered as it is passed on to others.

- *Refuse to assist apostasy.* The second letter of John contains a burning warning: "If there come any unto you, and bring not this doctrine [that is, the one gospel], receive him *not* into your house, neither bid him God speed: For he that biddeth him God speed is partaker of his evil deeds" (2 John 10-11, italics added). How easily we can slip over to Satan's side. We are to be ready to recognize apostasy, resist it, and refuse to assist it; but we are also called to something more.

- *Renew your love.* We are especially to renew our love for Jesus Christ. "Keep yourselves in the love of God," writes Jude (v. 21), as he closes his book on apostasy. Anything that comes between you and the Lord—any controversy, any unconfessed sin, any coolness—may be the first step toward apostasy.

Keeping yourself in the love of God means a close walk with Jesus Christ. It means daily obedience. It means feeding on the Word of God. It means not forsaking assembling together in the local church. It means being ready and watchful.

Someone has said the Christian life is like learning to ride a bicycle. If you want to keep upright, you have to keep going.

So walk on with the Lord today, tomorrow, and every day. Rejoice in Him. Contend for the faith. Watch and pray and serve—and He will keep you in the way of life everlasting.

"Now unto him that is able to keep you from falling, and to present you faultless before the presence of his glory with exceeding joy, to the only wise God our Saviour, be glory and majesty, dominion and power, both now and ever. Amen" (Jude 24-25).

4

Rapture

The Catching Away of the Church

> The trumpet of God will summon the dead in Christ to their resurrection and at the same time sound a warning to those who have rejected Christ that it is now too late to participate in the rapture. Clearly the rapture will *not* be a silent event.
> —Charles C. Ryrie

On July 20, 1969, astronauts Armstrong and Aldrin walked on the surface of the moon. Commander Neil Armstrong uttered the now famous words, "One small step for a man—one giant leap for mankind." But as incredible as that journey was, an event is coming that will truly leave mankind gaping in wonder.

News wires, broadcast services, and networks will tell the story of millions of people who suddenly and without warning simply vanished from the face of the earth while working, studying, driving, walking, eating, or sleeping. To the world in general it will be a mystery, but to Christians it will be another great prophecy fulfilled.

The event I am referring to, of course, is the removal of all believers from the earth—often called "the rapture." The word *rapture* does not appear in English versions of the Bible, but it comes from a Latin word that means "to catch

away" or "to seize." And although the word is not in the
Bible, the concept is clearly biblical. Scripture teaches that
Christ will return in the air to catch away all believers and
take them to be with Him forever. Like Enoch and Elijah of
the Old Testament, Christians will be translated, carried
away into the presence of God. This is the believer's hope.

First Corinthians 15:51-52 is a key text in describing the
rapture. There Paul writes to the Corinthians:

> Behold, I shew you a mystery; We shall not all sleep, but we
> shall all be changed, in a moment, in the twinkling of an eye,
> at the last trump: for the trumpet shall sound, and the dead
> shall be raised incorruptible, and we shall be changed.

"We shall not all sleep" is a promise that not all believers
will die. The apostle Paul frequently spoke of physical death
as sleep (1 Corinthians 15:18). Here he is proclaiming that a
day is coming when a whole generation of believers will be
raised out of their graves, and all Christians from every age
will be taken to be with the Lord forever in glorified bodies.
This event is a mystery, a formerly hidden truth now revealed in bold clarity.

The rapture will take only an instant. The word for "moment" in the Greek text refers to a period of time so small it
cannot be divided. Paul did not write "in the winking of an
eye," but rather "in the twinkling of an eye." This implies
instancy. The rapture will occur without warning at the last
trump—so fast that no one will see it happen.

The phrase *at the last trump* held a special significance for
the Jewish recipients of Paul's espistle. In the ancient Israelites' trek through the wilderness after leaving Egypt, they
knew it was time to move when a series of trumpets was
blown. Trumpets would sound to alert them to pack up
their things, take down their tents, and to get in formation
to move. When the last trumpet sounded, they knew it was
time to move in response to the leading of God.

The difference in the rapture is that the last trump will be
the *only* warning. Jesus could return now or at any moment
in the future. Those who are not believers will be left behind
to face the Tribulation.

For the believer, the rapture is a wonderful, comforting
truth. The apostle Paul wrote of it to the troubled Thessalonians, urging them to take comfort in his words:

But I would not have you to be ignorant, brethren, concerning them which are alseep, that ye sorrow not, even as others who have no hope. For if we believe that Jesus died and rose again, even so them also which sleep in Jesus will God bring with him. For this we say unto you by the word of the Lord, that we which are alive and remain unto the coming of the Lord shall not prevent [precede] them which are asleep. For the Lord himself shall descend from heaven with a shout, with the voice of the archangel, and with the trump of God: and the dead in Christ shall rise first: then we which are alive and remain shall be caught up together with them in the clouds to meet the Lord in the air: and so shall we ever be with the Lord. Wherefore, comfort one another with these words. (1 Thessalonians 4:13-18)

In that encouraging passage I see three outstanding truths that should be a comfort and inspiration to believers.

THE DEAD ARE RESTING

First is the truth that death is not final for believers. Paul says that those who have died in Christ are only asleep. In fact, it is only their bodies that are asleep, for they are with Christ (2 Corinthians 5:1-10; Philippians 1:21-23) and will return with Him when He comes to resurrect their bodies (1 Thessalonians 4:14).

Paul wrote to the Thessalonians because they were concerned about loved ones who had died. Each of them had looked forward to Christ's return, but they had died before the promise was fulfilled. The Thessalonians were not sure whether their loved ones would experience the Lord's return. Paul encouraged them, telling them that not only would those who had died in Christ be involved in the rapture, but that they would actually *rise first*.

It will be a great resurrection. The bodies of the dead will rise, transformed and glorified. "The dead shall be raised incorruptible, and we shall be changed," Paul writes in 1 Corinthians 15:52. Two events are involved here. One is the resurrection of the bodies of dead believers, and the other is the transformation of the bodies of all believers.

The transformation of the bodies of living believers is in itself a kind of resurrection. Paul writes in Romans 7:24, "O wretched man that I am! who shall deliver me from the body of this death?" First Thessalonians 4:13-18 is the answer to his own rhetorical question. He knew that the Lord Himself would descend and transform his body of death into a living, glorified body.

Describing the rapture to the Corinthians, Paul wrote, "For this corruptible must put on incorruption, and this mortal must put on immortality. So when this corruptible shall have put on incorruption, and this mortal shall have put on immortality, then shall be brought to pass the saying that is written, Death is swallowed up in victory" (1 Corinthians 15:53-54). That is what will happen in the rapture. That which is corruptible will put on incorruption, that which is mortal will put on immortality, and death will be swallowed up in victory.

A few years ago when I was in Northfield, Massachusetts to conduct evangelistic services, I visited "Roundtop" where D. L. Moody is buried. As I knelt in prayer, I recalled vividly Mr. Moody's eloquent words:

> Someday you will read in the papers that D. L. Moody is dead. Don't you believe a word of it. At that moment I shall have gone up higher; that is all; out of this old clay tenement, into a house that is immortal—a body that death cannot touch, that sin cannot taint; a body fashioned like unto His glorious body. I was born of the flesh in 1837. I was born of the spirit in 1856. That which is born of the flesh may die. That which is born of the spirit will live forever.[1]

Mr. Moody was right. And I expect to meet him one day in a glorified body that will never die.

THE LORD IS RETURNING

A second source of comfort is the truth that the Lord is returning. Paul says in 1 Thessalonians 4, "The Lord *himself* shall descend from heaven with a shout" (v. 16, italics added). He will return personally to receive us, just as He promised in John 14:3: "And if I go and prepare a place for you, I will come again, and receive you unto myself; that where I am, there ye may be also."

What a blessed hope that is for believers! He is coming in person for us. He will not send for us, or merely call to us,

---

1. *Cosmopolitan Magazine* 28 (March 1900): 510.

or just let us come to Him—He is coming in person to receive us.

Furthermore, when He comes He will bring our loved ones who died in Christ. We will have the inexpressible privilege of sharing eternity together with the redeemed of all ages, in the presence of the Lord Jesus Christ. What a wonderful time of reunion that will be!

THE PROMISE IS REASSURING

The final truth from 1 Thessalonians 4:13-18 is the knowledge that the promise of the rapture was given as reassurance. Paul told the Thessalonians to comfort one another with his words.

It is significant to note that Paul wrote to the Thessalonians to reassure them, because that substantiates two facts about the rapture. First, it is imminent. It could happen at any moment. It may seem like a contradiction to believe that something Paul wrote about almost two thousand years ago could have happened then at any moment and still might happen now at any moment, but it is not. No one knows the time of the Lord's return (Matthew 24:36), but it is the next event on God's prophetic calendar.

Second, the promise of the rapture indicates that believers will miss the Tribulation. The truth of the rapture would not have comforted the Thessalonians if they knew they would have to endure the Tribulation beforehand. Paul could not have told them to encourage and reassure each other with those truths if he knew they were facing the threat of the Tribulation.

Nowhere in Scripture are Christians told to prepare for the Tribulation. Believers are to look for the Lord's coming, not for God's judgment. First Thessalonians 5:4 states, "But ye, brethren, are not in darkness, that that day should overtake you as a thief." Verse nine continues to comfort: "For God hath not appointed us to wrath, but to obtain salvation by our Lord Jesus Christ." Thus Paul teaches that Jesus' return for believers at the rapture is a guarantee that they will not be among the objects of God's wrath as He pours out judgment on the world in the Tribulation.

As believers, we are to be sober, watchful, and faithful, living lives that are pleasing to Christ. No event or sign will precede His coming. He could come at any moment. It is not necessary to prepare for the Tribulation; we are simply to be ready for His imminent return.

The truth of the catching away of the church was important to my father. I remember him calling it to our attention as children. On one occasion after reading 1 Thessalonians chapter four, he quietly and methodically faced each of his six children with the question, "If Jesus returned tonight, would you be ready?" It was moving to hear each child answer, "Yes, I'm ready." Father then led us in singing the hymn "Will the Circle Be Unbroken When He Comes?" That is a question each individual must answer.

5

Reward

The Believer's Payday

Some seem to think that if we are Christians, God is not going
to bring up anything done in this life. It is all under the blood.
Put everything on Jesus and live any way you please. Surely
that cannot be right.

—Keith L. Brooks

If Jesus Christ returned today, the next event for the
Christian would be to stand before the judgment seat of
Christ. Judgment for believers is not a popular topic in this
age of "easy believism," but Scripture teaches that all believers will be judged. Second Corinthians 5:10 says, "For
we must all appear before the judgment seat of Christ; that
every one may receive the things done in his body, according to that he hath done, whether it be good or bad."

You may be thinking, *Salvation is by grace through faith,
and not of works. Why would God judge our works?* That is
an important question. Many people are confused about
what Scripture teaches regarding judgment. Biblically, no
judgment determines whether a person is saved or lost.
Salvation *is* by grace through faith, and salvation is estab-
lished and secured at the moment of faith. Judgment has
nothing to do with deciding whether a person will go to
heaven or hell.

Every judgment described in the Bible is a judgment of works. At the great white throne judgment, described in Revelation 20:11-15, the works of the unsaved dead will be judged. At the judgment seat of Christ, the works of believers will be judged. Rewards will be either lost or gained depending on the quality of the believer's works.

Why would God judge the works of believers? Let me suggest several reasons.

TO REVEAL THINGS THAT ARE HIDDEN

First, the judgment seat of Christ will bring to light things that are now hidden. True motives and characters will at that time be revealed. First Corinthians 3:13 says, "Every man's work shall be made manifest: for the day shall declare it, because it shall be revealed by fire; and the fire shall try every man's work of *what sort it is*" (italics added).

Jesus said, "There is nothing covered, that shall not be revealed; and hid, that shall not be known" (Matthew 10:26). And Paul warned, "Judge nothing before the time, until the Lord come, who both will bring to light the hidden things of darkness, and will make manifest the counsels of the hearts" (1 Corinthians 4:5).

That can be both reassuring and frightening. Misunderstandings will be cleared up, but hypocrisy will be exposed as well. Therefore those who have been falsely accused will be vindicated, whereas those who have been hypocritical will be unmasked. Disputes will be settled, conflicts will be resolved, and light will be shed on dark places. That which has been hidden will stand out in the white light of Christ's holy presence. It will be a sobering occasion.

TO RIGHT THAT WHICH IS WRONG

A second reason for the judgment of believers is to right that which is unjust or inequitable. Earthly judges may make errors, and justice is not always done in our courts; but Christ is one judge who cannot make a mistake. At the judgment seat of Christ, He will right all wrongs.

While I was in my first pastorate in New Jersey, my father-in-law passed away. He was a godly, consecrated man, respected and loved by those who knew him. More than three hundred of his friends came to his funeral to pay their respects. At the same time, a notorious crime figure in the area died. Thousands attended his funeral. My father-in-law's obituary took thirteen lines on page twenty-nine of the newspaper, but the crime figure's death was front-page news for more than a month.

That struck me as a perfect example of how erroneous worldly priorities are. Too often that which is truly important fades into the shadows of that which is spectacular. The people of God are ignored and often vilified, while those who are selfish, evil, or morally corrupt are portrayed as heroes.

But a day is coming when all of that will be made right. Justice—God's perfect justice—will be done, and He will reward us according to the truth (Romans 2:2). Romans 14:10, the only verse in the Bible besides 2 Corinthians 5:10 that mentions the judgment seat of Christ, says, "But why dost thou judge thy brother? or why dost thou set at nought thy brother? for we shall all stand before the judgment seat of Christ."

We do not need to judge and seek retribution, because we have the confidence that God will set all things right at the judgment seat.

TO REWARD THOSE WHO ARE WORTHY

Third, the judgment seat of Christ will reward those who are worthy. The Greek word for "judgment seat" is *bema*. A *bema* was a raised platform in an athletic arena, and victors in sporting events would stand before it to receive the rewards they had earned. Normally, the reward was a laurel wreath that was placed on the head of the winner.

The Corinthians understood the concept of the *bema* because their town was the location of the Isthmian games, an athletic competition that was held every two years and drew athletes from all over the world. In the center of the Corinthian agora was the *bema*. When not being used in sporting events, it was a speaker's stand or a magistrate's bench. It was before the Corinthian *bema* that Paul stood to be judged (Acts 18:12-13), and so his words had special significance to the Corinthians, many of whom may have remembered his appearance before the bench.

To the Corinthians, Paul writes, "We must all appear before the judgment seat [*bema*] of Christ; that every one may
receive the things done in his body, according to that he
hath done, whether it be good or bad" (2 Corinthians 5:10).
The "we" refers to Christians only; unbelievers' works will
be judged and punished, not rewarded, at the great white
throne judgment. Believers, however, will stand before the
bema, like victors in an athletic contest, to be rewarded.

It was a thrill for me to attend the 1972 and the 1976
Olympic Games. I remember the sensation that swept
through the crowd at the beginning of a race. Eight men
were off, running, pacing, and pressing themselves; and
only three would be honored. The winner received a gold
medal; the second-place finisher received a silver medal;
and the third-place contestant received a bronze medal. The
rest stood and watched and applauded.

Paul often used the athletic contest as a symbol for the
Christian life. In 1 Corinthians 9:24-27, he wrote:

> Know ye not that they which run in a race run all, but one
> receiveth the prize? So run, that ye may obtain. And every
> man that striveth for the mastery is temperate in all things.
> Now they do it to obtain a corruptible crown; but we an
> incorruptible. I therefore so run, not as uncertainly; so fight I,
> not as one that beateth the air: but I keep under my body, and
> bring it into subjection: lest that by any means, when I have
> preached to others, I myself should be a castaway.

Like the contestants in an Olympic race, we will either be
rewarded for how we have run or be left on the sidelines to
cheer. The differences are that we are competing not against
others but against the world, the flesh, and the devil; and
our crown is incorruptible. We seek it not for the praise of
men but for the glory of God.

Paul describes the judgment of works in 1 Corinthians
3:13-15:

> Every man's work shall be made manifest: for the day shall
> declare it, because it shall be revealed by fire; and the fire
> shall try every man's work of what sort it is. If any man's work
> abide which he hath built thereupon, he shall receive a re-
> ward. If any man's work shall be burned, he shall suffer loss:
> but he himself shall be saved; yet so as by fire.

Works of gold, silver, and precious stones will survive the fire, as opposed to works of wood, hay, and stubble (v. 12). The differences between such works are significant.

First, wood, hay, and stubble are perishable. Cast into the fire, they burn up. They are not lasting elements. That is not true of gold, silver, and precious stones. Fire refines them; only their impurities are burned up within it. That is true of our works as well. We need to be certain that we do things that count for eternity. It is easy to get caught up in temporal matters that seem urgent now but really are of no eternal consequence. If we are to be rewarded at the judgment seat, we need to take care to labor for things that count for eternity.

Second, wood, hay, and stubble can be easily manufactured. If you cut down a tree to make lumber, you can easily plant another tree to grow in its place. After harvesting the hay crop, you can always plant more. Those are resources that can be renewed with human effort. But gold, silver, and precious stones cannot be created or reproduced by any amount of human effort. They have to be mined instead of harvested, and they are not unlimited in supply. A believer's works are like that. If they are the product of his own efforts, no matter how good they look externally they will be burned up. But if they are done in the power of the Holy Spirit, they will last forever.

True spirituality cannot be created or reproduced by human effort. It is the product of a heart completely consecrated to God, wholly yielded to the Holy Spirit, and fully controlled by Jesus Christ. True spirituality alone can produce the works of gold, silver, and precious stones that will be rewarded before the *bema*.

Consider your life. Are you building with gold, silver, and precious stones, or with hay, wood, and stubble? Will the judgment seat of Christ mean gain or loss for you? Even as a believer, the quality of your life will have eternal consequences. Are you living in the light of His coming? Does the promise of judgment hold fear or rejoicing for you?

A Christian dreamed he stood before the judgment seat of Christ. As he looked on in wonder, all the worthwhile things he had done since accepting Christ were brought and placed before the Son of God. There was his singing in various services—and his years of teaching in Sunday school. All his giving, all his kindnesses, and all his personal efforts as a Christian were brought before the Lord.

While he watched, all these things were placed together in a giant test tube. A flame was lit beneath, and as the products of his life were heated they began to melt and separate on different levels in the tube.

Only then did he realize what was taking place. The Divine Chemist began to measure the separated contents—the motives that had prompted his years of service.

Carefully he watched while the first measurement was made. Love of praise, 20 percent! Sense of responsibility came next; that measured 25 percent. Hypocrisy, 15 percent; personal ambition, 20 percent . . .

At last the final figure was written out before him. It struck him like a blow. Only 20 percent of all that he had done had come from an unaffected love for Christ. Then he awoke from his dream.

The Bible makes clear that the judgment seat of Christ for the Christian is not a dream. It is a part of God's program and God's purpose.

Now is the time to right things that are wrong and to reveal things that are hidden. Scripture advises, "If we would judge ourselves, we should not be judged" (1 Corinthians 11:31). I urge you to make things right in your life right now, so that at the judgment seat of Christ you can be counted worthy of reward.

6

Rebellion

The Antichrist and the Tribulation

Antichrist is so proud, as to go before Christ; so humble as to pretend to come after him; and so audacious as to say that himself is he.

—John Bunyan

.The world is looking for a powerful leader—an international figure to offer practical solutions to the world's problems of war, suffering, hunger, and pestilence. Weary of hollow promises, people want a tried and proved superleader, a shining knight strong enough to guarantee peace.

In the world today, international leaders change with amazing speed. Looking back over the past ten years, we see that the roster of leaders who were in power ten years ago and still are today is incredibly short. They have been removed from power by resignation, assassination, revolution, and death, and often their power base crumbles with their passing. Those who succeed them often blur their predecessor's achievements and discredit his words; then they fall from power just as quickly.

It is into this kind of political atmosphere that the Antichrist will come. He will offer peace and prosperity, but ultimately he will threaten the very existence of civilization. His power will be so complete and evil that only Jesus Christ will be able to conquer him and free the world from his grip, thereby bringing down the curtain on the present age.

THE REVELATION OF ANTICHRIST

In 2 Thessalonians, Paul writes of the Antichrist, calling him "that man of sin . . . the son of perdition; who opposeth and exalteth himself above all that is called God, or that is worshipped" (2 Thessalonians 2:3-4). Thus, according to Paul, the Antichrist will set himself in the place of God and demand that he be worshipped.

The Antichrist cannot come right now, however, for he is being restrained. Paul went on to write, "And now ye know what withholdeth that he might be revealed in his time. For the mystery of iniquity doth already work: only he who now letteth [restrains] will let [restrain], until he be taken out of the way. And then shall that Wicked be revealed" (2 Thessalonians 2:6-8). "He who now letteth" is the Holy Spirit, present among believers in the church age. But when the rapture takes all believers out of the world, nothing will keep the Antichrist from coming into power. Thus I believe his reign will begin shortly after the rapture.

The "son of perdition" will exhibit all the worst characteristics of evil leadership. He will be hypocritical, domineering, savage, and insane, completely controlled by the devil. Yet he will come to power on a promise of peace, claiming to be the Messiah of the Jews. Jesus said of him, "If another shall come in his own name, him ye will receive" (John 5:43). Promising peace to Israel, he will make a covenant with them: "And he shall confirm the covenant with many for one week [seven years]" (Daniel 9:27).

First Thessalonians 5:3, however, warns that the peace will not last long. "For when they shall say, Peace and safety; then sudden destruction cometh upon them." Antichrist will suddenly break his covenant by desecrating the Temple (Daniel 9:27), and then will begin the worst campaign of terror and persecution the Jewish people have ever seen.

At the same time, God will pour out His wrath on the world for its rebellion. Natural disasters, supernatural chastisement, war, and pestilence will hit the world in wave after wave of divine judgment. Yet Antichrist and the world he controls will remain steadfast in their rebellion against God.

The word *Antichrist* means "one who stands against Christ," and he will do just that. After he has deceived the world into accepting his rule, he will abuse his power and oppose and exalt himself against God, even to the point of sitting "in the temple of God, shewing himself that he is God" (2 Thessalonians 2:4).

THE POWER OF ANTICHRIST

To accomplish such widespread deception, the Antichrist will derive his amazing supernatural power directly from Satan, the god of this world, prince of the power of the air. Satan once offered Christ control over all the kingdoms of the world if only He would bow down and worship him (Matthew 4:8-10). The Lord rejected that offer, so Satan will now give control of the earth to one whom he can control.

Antichrist's power will extend to every area of life in every part of the world. His dictatorship will be religious, political, and economic. He will have supernatural abilities, including the power to counterfeit miracles.

He will come as an angel of light. But clearly his "coming is after the working of Satan with all power and signs and lying wonders" (2 Thessalonians 2:9). And the world—intent on having a leader, even if it means denying God's choice—will be so deluded that it will accept him. "Because they received not the love of the truth, that they might be saved. And for this cause God shall send them strong delusion, that they should believe [the] lie" (2 Thessalonians 2:10-11).

In order to consolidate his reign, Antichrist will set up a false religious system. He will utilize the power of a satanic false prophet, and together they will demand that people forsake every other religion. True believers in Christ will resist the pressure to bow to this evil falsehood, but the price will be martyrdom.

THE TIME OF ANTICHRIST

The time during which the Antichrist will control the earth is known as the Tribulation. In Scripture it is sometimes called "the day of the Lord" (Joel 1:15; Amos 5:18; Zephaniah 1:14); "the day of his fierce anger" (Isaiah 13:13); "the time of Jacob's trouble" (Jeremiah 30:7); and "the tribulation" (Matthew 24:29).

It will be a terrible time of war, famine, death, and earth-quakes (Revelation 6:4-8, 12), as well as various other disasters and judgments. A large portion of humanity will be killed as God pours out His wrath and Satan works out his oppression. Still, men's hearts will be hardened as they refuse to repent and even curse God in the midst of their judgment.

Yet some will be saved. God will raise up two witnesses who will point to the way of truth. "And I will give power unto my two witnesses, and they shall prophesy a thousand two hundred and threescore days, clothed in sackcloth" (Revelation 11:3). They will have supernatural powers to confirm their message:

> If any man will hurt them, fire proceedeth out of their mouth, and devoureth their enemies: and if any man will hurt them, he must in this manner be killed. These have power to shut heaven, that it rain not in the days of their prophecy: and have power over waters to turn them to blood, and to smite the earth with all plagues, as often as they will. (Revelation 11:5-6)

These two witnesses will be testimonies to the world in the midst of darkness. But they will so arouse the wrath of the Antichrist that he will be determined to annihilate them. Ultimately, he will have his way. "When they shall have finished their testimony, the beast that ascendeth out of the bottomless pit shall make war against them, and shall overcome them, and kill them" (Revelation 11:7).

Perhaps to show the world his power, the Antichrist will display the bodies of the two witnesses to all the world. "And their dead bodies shall lie in the street of the great city. . . And they of the people and kindreds and tongues and nations shall see their dead bodies three days and an half, and shall not suffer their dead bodies to be put in graves" (Revelation 11:8-9). A great rejoicing will sweep over the earth at the death of the two witnesses, whom the world will have perceived as the source of all the suffering. But after lying in the street dead, in full view of everyone, the two witnesses will suddenly be brought back to life and translated.

At that point, the greatest judgments of all will be poured out on the earth. Revelation 16 describes how God will pour out seven vials of judgment on the wicked. Those who worship the Antichrist will be infected with sores. The sea will turn like "the blood of a dead man" (v. 3), and all life in it will perish; rivers and other fresh water will become blood, the sun will become scorching, darkness will descend, and finally God will say, "It is done" (v. 17). Then a great earthquake and huge hailstones will destroy much of what is left of the Antichrist's kingdom.

As evil and corrupt as the Tribulation will be, it nevertheless will be a time when God will be reaching out in grace and offering salvation to those who will believe. Through all the wrath and persecution that is poured out upon Israel, the believing remnant will remain pure by the power of God during this time. Despite martyrdom, persecution, and the power of the Antichrist, many will come to faith in Christ. God's program of offering salvation to all who believe will continue.

THE END OF ANTICHRIST

Seven years may not seem like a long time for an empire to last, but it is enough time for unchecked evil to work itself to its ultimate end. Finally, God will call a halt to the Antichrist's wicked reign. It will all culminate in a great and final battle on the plains of Megiddo, where the Antichrist and his evil forces will come together to wage war against God.

The Antichrist, deluded by Satan, will imagine that he can actually defeat Christ in this final battle. His hate and blasphemy against God will focus on believing Israel, and he will mount one final offensive to destroy the remnant of the Jews. It is in the middle of that final battle that Christ will return to defeat all the forces of evil. And He will do so merely with the brightness of His appearing and through the power of His Word (2 Thessalonians 2:8).

The culmination of the Antichrist's reign will be when he is cast into the lake of fire, where he will be judged forever with eternal torment. He will receive the just reward for his rebellion against God.

Yet we have a God of mercy. He offers salvation to those who will yield to Him, and He is patient with those who sin. But we must be careful not to become hardened in rebellion against Him. If we learn anything from studying the Antichrist's career, it is that when rebellion runs its full course it ultimately proves to be futile. God cannot be mocked, and His holiness is infinite. We dare not take His mercy and love for granted. And we dare not yield to or worship anything, or anyone, other than Him.

7

Rebirth

The Nation Israel—Past, Present, and Future

Certainly as Israel's promises are being fulfilled before our eyes other aspects of prophecy such as the resurrection of the dead in Christ and the translation of living saints become a real and an imminent possibility.

—John F. Walvoord

No nation is more significant in the future of world politics than the nation of Israel. That is a meaningful statement in light of the fact that less than fifty years ago some believed that the Jewish people could never again hope to return to their land as a sovereign nation. Today the headlines show that what was once scoffed at as a ludicrous idea has indeed taken place. Israel has returned to the world scene and is now more important, more strategic, and more crucial to future events than ever seemed possible. The rebirth of the nation Israel has been like the key piece of a jigsaw puzzle, enabling the other pieces to fall quickly in place.

No story in all of human history is as heroic as that of the Jewish race. Throughout history, God's chosen people have suffered greatly. Yet as we study the Bible and the past, we find that God has also blessed them in a unique way.

More than any other of the world's races and nations, the Jewish people can trace their history with accuracy. The origin of most nations is wrapped in surmise and conjecture, but Scripture clearly records the beginning of the Hebrews. In Genesis 12, the Lord said to Abraham, "Get thee out of thy country, and from thy kindred, and from thy father's house, unto a land that I will shew thee: And I will make of thee *a great nation,* and I will bless thee, and make thy name great; and thou shalt be a blessing: and I will bless them that bless thee, and curse him that curseth thee: and in thee shall all families of the earth be blessed" (vv. 1-3, italics added).

That promise of God to Abraham sums up God's plan for the Jewish race. As the chosen people of God, they became a great nation. Through them all the other nations of the earth have been blessed, because it was through the nation of Israel that God gave us revelation about Himself, the Scriptures, and ultimately His Son, Jesus Christ.

Over the centuries the Jewish people have been scattered throughout the world, living with persecution and oppression. Yet God has faithfully blessed those who have blessed the Jews and cursed those who have persecuted them. A list of the persecutions of the Jews since 1000 B.C. would be many pages long, but just as God promised Abraham, every nation that has persecuted the Israelites has passed from the world scene; every ruler who has oppressed them has been deposed; and every society that has abused them has fallen.

Perhaps the most incredible thing of all is that despite all the opposition, persecution, attempts of wicked rulers to stamp them out, and the fact that they have been scattered for centuries among all nations, the Hebrew people have retained their identity as a distinct nation.

Although God's plan for Israel was for them to remain in the Promised Land and be His representative people on the earth, He warned them from the beginning that they would be set aside if they were not faithful to Him. God prophesied through Moses that the Jewish people would be scattered abroad into all the nations for their rebelliousness. Deuteronomy 28:64 says, "And the Lord shall scatter thee among all people, from the one end of the earth even unto the other."

The chosen people were scattered because they turned away from God. Romans 11:20 explains, "Because of unbelief they were broken off." Having rejected their Redeemer, they were set aside while God in this age calls out a people for Himself from all nations. The Promised Land was taken over by Gentiles, and God's people were expelled.

To understand how devastating the dispersion was to the Hebrew nation, it helps to understand the Jewish sacrificial system. All worship took place at one central location—the Temple in Jerusalem. When a Jewish person wished to worship God with a sacrifice or an offering, he could not go to a local altar; he had to go to Jerusalem. The local synagogues were centers of teaching, not places for ceremonial worship.

Thus, the religion of ancient Israel was closely tied to the geography of the land. Jerusalem was uphill from every other location. It sat overlooking the Promised Land, drawing the entire nation together in the worship of its God. The city and the Temple were the pinnacle of the nation's social, religious, economic, and political life, central to everything else.

When Jerusalem was overrun by Rome in A.D. 70, the Temple was destroyed. That signaled the end of the Jewish religion as it had been known, the end of Israel as a political force, and ultimately the end of Jewish habitation of Palestine. From a human standpoint, it seemed that the nation of Israel had been destroyed forever.

Still, throughout all the years of dispersion the Jews held the hope of returning to the land that God promised to their Fathers. Every year, each Jewish family that observes the Passover feast ends the ritual with the words "Next year in Jerusalem."

Incredibly, centuries after the dispersion, the modern state of Israel officially came into being on May 15, 1948. In our lifetime, we are seeing the people of Israel return to their homeland from all the nations of the earth just as Scripture prophesied. In the face of unbelievable odds, this

tiny nation has grown in a few decades to become a domi-
nating force in the Middle East. And with these events, the
stage is being set for the ultimate fulfillment of God's purpose for Israel, His people.

THE RETURN OF ISRAEL

There is a bright and exciting future for the nation of
Israel. Jeremiah 31:10 says, "He that scattered Israel will
gather him." God is going to continue bringing the people
of Israel back to their land for the fulfillment of the promises He made to Abraham many years ago. The Jewish nation, despite the stated intentions of many of her enemies, is
indestructible. This is God's promise: "I am with thee, saith
the Lord, to save thee: though I make a full end of all
nations whither I have scattered thee, yet will I not make a
full end of thee" (Jeremiah 30:11).

One of the great passages in the Bible concerning Israel is
the vision of the prophet found in Ezekiel 37:1-10. It tells of
a valley full of scattered, dried bones that come together
and are restored to life. It is symbolic of the regeneration of
Israel in the end times. In many ways, the prophecy seems
to be being fulfilled before our very eyes. The deepest
meaning of the prophecy, however, will be fulfilled at the
second coming of Christ.

It is significant that Ezekiel's vision took place in a valley.
In a striking picture of Israel's history, the scattered bones
symbolize dispersed Israel in a two-thousand-year-long valley of suffering and tragedy, seemingly too lifeless to be
anything but tragic reminders of a once glorious people of
God. Ezekiel states that the bones "were very dry" (v. 2),
having been subjected to years of exposure from the light
they had rejected.

The picture is one of hopelessness, death, despair, and
decay. And thus it has been for God's chosen nation for the
past two millennia.

For years, many said that the rebirth of the nation Israel
was an impossibility. Yet it is happening right now as Jewish
people from all over the world return to their homeland by
the millions. The sinew and the flesh of national organiza-
tion have bound the bones together. Meanwhile, the desert
is starting to blossom, and the land is being reclaimed. Isra-

el has repeatedly proved to the world it is a nation that must be reckoned with.

Let me be clear. The restoration we are seeing in Israel today is not the complete fulfillment of Ezekiel 37. The rebirth spoken of there is spiritual, in which the nation will experience the new birth of salvation when the people embrace their Messiah. But the political rebirth we are witnessing may be the beginning of the fulfillment of that great prophecy. In light of what is occurring on the world scene today, can our Lord's return be very far away?

Scripture reveals that Israel is the place where the last great conflict will take place. As the enemy prepares for that confrontation, it is not accidental that the key tensions of our time center in the Middle East.

Zechariah 14:1-4 is significant in its description of the return of our Lord to the earth.

> Behold, the day of the Lord cometh, and thy spoil shall be divided in the midst of thee. For I will gather all nations against Jerusalem to battle; and the city shall be taken, and the houses rifled, and the women ravished; and half of the city shall go forth into captivity, and the residue of the people shall not be cut off from the city. Then shall the Lord go forth, and fight against those nations, as when he fought in the day of battle. And his feet shall stand in that day upon the mount of Olives, which is before Jerusalem on the east, and the mount of Olives shall cleave in the midst thereof toward the east and toward the west, and there shall be a very great valley; and half of the mountain shall remove toward the north, and half of it toward the south.

The passage reveals that the place Christ will return to is the Mount of Olives, near Jerusalem, where He prayed the night He was betrayed. And it was from there that Christ ascended to heaven, and an angel appeared to the watching disciples to say, "Ye men of Galilee, why stand ye gazing up into heaven? this same Jesus, which is taken up from you into heaven, shall so come in like manner as ye have seen him go into heaven" (Acts 1:11).

That promise may be fulfilled at any time, and nothing points to its quick fulfillment more than the return of the nation Israel to the land.

If God is able to make dry bones come together and live

again, if He is able to restore a scattered nation to world prominence, and if He is able to oversee world events in the midst of today's chaos to bring about the fulfillment of two-thousand-year-old prophecies, He is certainly able to redeem anyone who comes to Him in repentant faith.

8

Resurrection

A Matter of Death and Life

The resurrection that awaits us beyond physical death will be but the glorious consummation of the risen life which already we have in Christ.

—D. T. Niles

Death touches all of us, yet few people understand what Scripture teaches concerning it. Many rely on superstition and false hopes, facing eternity with little or no real thought. In fact, our society as a whole views death as an unpleasant and undesirable topic, better ignored than confronted.

But to ignore death and the hereafter is a mistake, for Scripture reads, "It is appointed unto men once to die, but after this the judgment" (Hebrews 9:27).

Life for you may be like a long day in June or it may be like a short day in February. But long or short, early or late, like it or not, everyone must die. Death is a fact of life. Statisticians tell us that over ninety people die every minute—more than fifty-four hundred every hour.

EVERYONE WILL DIE

The language of Hebrews 9:27 suggests that death is a divine appointment we cannot escape. That inescapability is also illustrated in the story of a certain Eastern merchant who sent his servant to the city of Baghdad to buy provisions. While in the marketplace, the servant saw the figure of Death, and Death seemed to point at him.

Gripped with fear, the servant hurried back to his master and said, "Master, today at the marketplace in Baghdad I saw the figure of Death; and Death pointed at me. Give me your horse and let me escape to the far-off town of Samara, and there Death will not find me." And so the servant fled to Samara.

Later that day, the merchant went to the marketplace in Baghdad. Seeing the figure of Death there, he asked, "Why did you threaten my servant this morning?"

"Oh," replied Death, "that was not a threatening gesture; that was a start of surprise. I was astonished to see him here in the marketplace in Baghdad, because tonight I have an appointment with him in Samara."

Plan as you will, everyone has an appointment with death that cannot be avoided.

God did not create man to die, though. Death is a result of disobedience and rebellion. The first man, Adam, was placed in a perfect environment. God instructed him that he could eat the fruit of any tree in the Garden except for the tree of the knowledge of good and evil. Adam willfully disobeyed the command of God, following his will instead of God's.

After his disobedience, God said to Adam, "In the sweat of thy face shalt thou eat bread, till thou return unto the ground; for out of it wast thou taken: for dust thou art, and unto dust shalt thou return" (Genesis 3:19).

Not only was Adam judged, but his sinful nature was passed on to future generations as well. All mankind became sinners; thus, Adam and all his offspring were subject to death. In Romans 5:12 Paul writes, "Wherefore, as by one man sin entered into the world, and death by sin; and so death passed upon all men, for that all have sinned." We are sinners by nature and by choice.

In his book *The End Times*, Herman Hoyt writes: "The

entire person is involved in the experience of physical death. This includes spirit, soul, and body."[1] When an individual dies, there is a dissolution of the parts of that person—the body is separated from the soul and spirit.

Physical death is a fulfillment of God's judgment upon man because of his sin. Genesis 3:19 and Romans 5:12 state it plainly. But there is a remedy for sin, and there is a way out from the fear of death. It is the gift of eternal life that is freely given to those who trust in Jesus Christ (Romans 6:23).

Jesus Christ died for our sin, was buried, and rose again the third day according to the Scriptures. The death and resurrection of Jesus Christ is God's cure for sin and death: because of His death and triumphant resurrection, we know there is life after death. Those who have been redeemed through faith in Christ will live forever with Him. For believers in Jesus Christ, death is not the end. It is not an annihilation, a blank nothingness. Rather, it is a triumphal entry into God's presence.

When D. L. Moody was dying, he expressed neither fear nor anguish. As his family gathered quietly about him, he said, "If this is death, it is sweet. . . . Don't call me back. This is my coronation day. This is the day I've dreamed of." Then he beautifully and quietly fell asleep in Jesus.

That is how the New Testament describes death—as a falling asleep in Jesus—because that is what it is. It is not the end but the beginning of a new life forever with Christ. I like the way the psalmist David referred to death as "the valley of the shadow of death" (Psalm 23:4). It is the *shadow* of death. The shadow of a gun cannot shoot you, the shadow of a knife cannot cut you, and the shadow of a dog cannot bite you. Likewise, the shadow of death holds no eternal threat for the trusting child of God.

That is why Paul could write, "Knowing that he which raised up the Lord Jesus shall raise up us also by Jesus" (2 Corinthians 4:14). He also wrote in 2 Corinthians 5:1, "For we know that if our earthly house . . . were dissolved, we have . . . an house not made with hands, eternal in the heavens." Paul was confident concerning his eternal future. For him the fear of death was removed forever by the resur-

1. Herman Hoyt, *The End Times* (Chicago: Moody, 1969), p. 24.

rected Christ. And those who through Christ have received eternal life can join Paul in saying, "O death, where is thy sting? O grave, where is thy victory?" (1 Corinthians 15:55).

After death, believers live on with Christ, and a great day of resurrection is coming when their spirits will be reunited with glorified, redeemed bodies, free of sin and death forever. That is why death is not such a frightening subject for Christians. We need not fear death, for it is the beginning of our eternal existence with the Lord (Philippians 1:23).

EVERYONE WILL BE RAISED FROM THE DEAD

Many people do not understand that death is not the end of existence for anyone. Remember, "It is appointed unto men once to die, but after this the judgment" (Hebrews 9:27). No one will be exempt from that judgment after death. Even those who die without Christ will be resurrected *to face judgment*.

First Corinthians 15 is the definitive New Testament chapter on resurrection. In it, Paul argues that faith in the fact that Jesus rose from the dead is a fundamental element of Christianity.

> But now is Christ risen from the dead, and become the firstfruits of them that slept. For since by man came death, by man came also the resurrection of the dead. For as in Adam all die, even so in Christ shall all be made alive. But every man in his own order: Christ the firstfruits; afterward they that are Christ's at his coming. Then cometh the end, when he shall have delivered up the kingdom to God. (1 Corinthians 15:20-24)

That passage teaches several important truths about resurrection. First, Paul says that all men will be resurrected. In the same way that death came to all mankind through the act of the man Adam, resurrection also comes to humanity through the act of the man Jesus.

But notice that resurrection is not the same for every man. There is an order to resurrection; and every man will be raised "in his own order" (v. 23). Christ was first, and He will be followed in resurrection by those who are His. That resurrection will take place when He comes—at the rapture, when "the dead in Christ shall rise" (1 Thessalonians 4:16).

The dead who did not trust Christ will be resurrected as well. In Revelation 20:12, the apostle John describes that awesome sight: "And I saw the dead, small and great, stand before God; and the books were opened: and another book was opened, which is the book of life: and the dead were judged out of those things which were written in the books, according to their works."

That resurrection is solely for the purpose of judgment. And it appears to be a bodily resurrection, not merely disembodied souls standing before God to be judged. Verse 13 goes on to say, "And the sea gave up the dead which were in it; and death and hell delivered up the dead which were in them: and they were judged every man according to their works." The dead are actually brought up from the grave to face this awful judgment.

This resurrection is separate and vastly different from the resurrection of believers. Whereas believers are raised to eternal life, these people are raised to face a second—eternal—death: "And death and hell were cast into the lake of fire. *This is the second death.* And whosoever was not found written in the book of life was cast into the lake of fire" (Revelation 20:14-15, italics added).

EVERYONE MUST MAKE THE CHOICE

Everyone, then, must die; and everyone will be resurrected. Jesus said, "Marvel not at this: for the hour is coming, in the which all that are in the graves shall hear his voice, and shall come forth; they that have done good, unto the resurrection of life; and they that have done evil, unto the resurrection of damnation" (John 5:28-29). Which resurrection you face is determined in this life. That is why it is folly to refuse to face the issue of death and the afterlife. The question of your eternity is the most significant issue you will confront.

In Luke 16, Jesus gives a telling account of two men who died. The differences in their earthly lives and their eternal states make a shocking contrast. One was an unnamed rich man who loved fine clothes and good food and lived with little thought of death. He was well taken care of in this life but ill-prepared for the next. The other man was a beggar named Lazarus, who lived with dogs and ate the crumbs off the rich man's table. Nevertheless, he was redeemed and thus prepared for what faced him after death.

Both men died. The rich man went to hell; and Lazarus was carried by angels into paradise. The rich man in his torments cried out, "Father Abraham, have mercy on me, and send Lazarus, that he may dip the tip of his finger in water, and cool my tongue; for I am tormented in this flame" (Luke 16:24). When told that was not possible, the rich man asked for Lazarus to be sent back from the dead to warn his brothers so they would not also be cast into hell. Abraham's answer indicts all unbelievers: "They have Moses and the prophets; let them hear them. . . . If they hear not Moses and the prophets, neither will they be persuaded, though one rose from the dead" (Luke 16:29, 31).

One *has* risen from the dead—the same One who died for our sins. Because Christ died as a perfect sacrifice, He has purchased eternal life for us. All He requires is that we trust in Him with sincere, repentant faith. We do not have to *earn* eternal life—He offers it freely as a gift, and those who receive it become new creatures, formed in His image.

Only a fool would reject such an offer. But to neglect it is to reject it, and many are guilty of that neglect. Many will be in the resurrection of damnation simply because they did not make the choice when they had the opportunity. You can be as sure of heaven as though you were already there by sincerely committing yourself to Jesus Christ and His salvation.

9

Restoration

The Millennium

> As the world hath seen the manner of the reign of Antichrist, and how tyrannical and outrageous a kingdom his is; so they shall see the reign of Christ, by his word and Spirit in his people, how peaceable, how fruitful in blessedness and prosperity his kingdom is.
>
> —John Bunyan

Despite the scientific and technological advances of the past few decades, our world could be a harder place to live in by the year 2,000. A recent study issued by the President's Council on Environmental Quality predicts that continued population growth and resource depletion will result in a progressive degradation and impoverishment of the earth's natural resources.

According to the study, millions of people will be undernourished, air and water quality will deteriorate, agricultural lands will erode, and vast forests will become barren. These experts see world population increasing by 50 percent to about 6 billion people by the year 2000. But food output will increase, they estimate, only 15 percent. Worldwide hunger may threaten mankind's very existence. Some are convinced that human life is threatened as never before in the history of this planet, not just by one peril, but by many.

What is wrong with our world? Why can't something be done to get it back in order? The answer is that human sin has been destroying our world ever since Adam's Fall. Little can be done to save it until evil is completely defeated in the hearts of men, in the governments that determine the course of society, and in the spiritual realm that covers the world as we know it.

Yet the world is not without hope, for Jesus Christ has already won the ultimate battle over evil principalities and powers and will one day return to set all things right on the earth. In spite of the evil and rebellion that threaten to consume our world, a great day is coming. Jesus Christ will live and rule on the earth, and the world will acknowledge Him as King. For one thousand years He will reign, bringing peace to the world and salvation and prosperity to Israel. It will be the perfect society we have only dreamed of.

THE QUEST FOR UTOPIA

Almost from the beginning of history, man has been trying to establish the perfect society. The tower of Babel represents an attempt to unite the world in one society with a single religion and a common language. The people decided to build a great tower to symbolize their purpose. But the religion was paganism, and the basis of their unity was rebellion against God and His purposes. Therefore God confounded their language and forced the dissolution of their society.

History is filled with accounts of men, rulers, and organizations who believed they held the secret to world unity through religion, government, or some other human endeavor. At best these men had good intentions but little knowledge of the true God; at worst they were wicked oppressors, like Nero.

Human effort could never bring about world peace or unity—and certainly not a Utopia. The problem is the sin within each man. All of mankind is in rebellion against God. The human depravity we see all around us is a result of the Fall of Genesis 3, brought about because of Adam's revolt against God.

The manifestations of that revolt may be more visible today than ever before in the history of man. They include such symptoms as the violation of natural resources, nations warring against nations, poverty and disease, hatred and strife, the strong devouring the weak, the growing divorce rate, the breakdown of the family, and most of all, the spirit of selfishness that says "I'll do what I want to do." Personal and corporate crime abound. Pornography and sexual immorality are viewed by many as normal and acceptable. Leaders fall from positions of authority. Our newspapers are filled with accounts of murder, crime, war, divorce, illness, failure, poverty, and pollution. A spirit of anarchy prevails.

However well intended, every human attempt at the perfect society is grounded in rebellion against God. The psalmist asks, "Why do the heathen rage, and the people imagine a vain thing? The kings of the earth set themselves, and the rulers take counsel together, against the Lord, and against his anointed, saying, Let us break their bands asunder, and cast away their cords from us" (Psalm 2:1-3).

Christ told a parable about a nobleman whose subjects despised him. Luke 19:14 says they jeered defiantly, "We will not have this man to reign over us." That is the attitude of the mass of mankind today: "We will not have God rule over us." Though men may scoff, resist His truth, and attempt to build their own kingdoms, every earthly kingdom is destined for failure. No human attempt to bring about Utopia can ever succeed, for the human heart has set itself against God.

THE REJECTION OF MESSIAH

The promise of a millennial kingdom was given to the nation of Israel almost three thousand years ago. Isaiah wrote much about this coming time of world peace:

> And it shall come to pass in the last days, that the mountain of the Lord's house shall be established in the top of the mountains, and shall be exalted above the hills; and all nations shall flow unto it. And many people shall go and say, Come ye, and let us go up to the mountain of the Lord, to the house of the God of Jacob; and he will teach us of his ways, and we will walk in his paths: for out of Zion shall go forth the law, and the word of the Lord from Jerusalem. And he shall judge among the nations, and shall rebuke many people: and they shall beat

their swords into plowshares, and their spears into pruning-hooks: nation shall not lift up sword against nation, neither shall they learn war any more. (Isaiah 2:2-4)

All Israel anticipated the time when they would be free of oppression, and their king—God's anointed ruler, the Messiah—would rule the whole world in righteousness and peace. They looked for Him diligently, expecting Him to be a conquering deliverer who would free them from the tyranny of Rome.

But when He came, announcing, "The kingdom of heaven is at hand" (Matthew 4:17), His message to the nation of Israel was that they should repent. Instead of preaching revolution, He preached holiness. And rather than overthrow Gentile oppression, He reached out to the Gentile people in love.

Jesus was not at all like the Messiah the Jewish people were looking for. They sought a political leader; His message was spiritual. They expected a victorious warrior; He died with condemned criminals. They hoped for someone who would deliver them from the oppression of the Romans; He came to deliver them from the oppression of their own sin.

So the Israelites rejected their Savior and King. They rejected His message, His kingdom, and His person. "We will not have this man to rule over us!" And because the nation of Israel denied Christ His rightful place, the kingdom was postponed. In this age God has turned to the Gentiles, "to take out of them a people for his name" (Acts 15:14).

THE FULFILLMENT OF THE PROMISE

Numbers 23:19 says, "God is not a man, that he should lie; neither the son of man, that he should repent: hath he said, and shall he not do it? or hath he spoken, and shall he not make it good?" The promise of a kingdom here on earth is not symbolic. Jesus *will* set up rule on earth and put down all rebellion. He *will* right the wrongs of the world. He *will* rule with love and justice. He *will* bring the world out of its present state and create a new order based on His unchangeable character.

Israel will receive Jesus as her Messiah, and the millennial kingdom will be ushered in at the close of the Tribulation. Christ will return to defeat the Antichrist and the enemies of Israel with the redeemed of the church age, and the false prophet and the Antichrist will be judged with the nations. The Millennium will begin.

Christ's authority comes from God the Father, and He will rule as a servant appointed by God. In Isaiah 42:1, God speaks of Christ as "My servant, whom I uphold; mine elect, in whom my soul delighteth; I have put my spirit upon him: he shall bring forth judgment to the Gentiles." Christ as Lord and King will serve with both human and divine authority. He is "a rod out of the stem of Jesse" (Isaiah 11:1) and "the Son of man" (Daniel 7:13). But Scripture also indicates that He is "the mighty God" (Isaiah 9:6).

Therein is the reason only Christ can usher in the Millennium: He alone can serve as mediator between God and man. As both God and man He is able to represent mankind to God. But he also acts for God the Father with His people, serving as a prophet to deliver the words of God to His subjects. He will be a priest ministering to the spiritual needs of His people; He will also be a king ruling with justice unheard of in the present age.

The Lord Jesus Christ will bring to His throne a perfect character that no ruler on earth has ever possessed. Isaiah said, "The spirit of the Lord shall rest upon him, the spirit of wisdom and understanding, the spirit of counsel and might, the spirit of knowledge and of the fear of the Lord" (Isaiah 11:2). He will have sole authority for the conduct of His government. Isaiah 9:6 says of Christ, "The government shall be upon his shoulder." While others will have delegated responsibilities within the kingdom, it is Christ who will make it all work.

He will rule with a "rod of iron" (Psalm 2:7-9), but He also will continue to minister with the compassion and gentleness of a shepherd. Listen to Isaiah 40:11: "He shall gather the lambs with his arm, and carry them in his bosom, and shall gently lead those that are with young."

The millennial kingdom will be a revival and continuation of the historic kingdom of David. Israel will be the seat of authority among the nations. She will at last enjoy the peace that she has sought for so long. That peace will bless the other peoples of the world as well: "Of the increase of his government and peace there shall be no end, upon the throne of David, and upon his Kingdom, to order it, and to establish it with judgment and with justice from henceforth even for ever" (Isaiah 9:7).

"The Lord shall be king over all the earth: in that day shall there be one Lord, and his name one" (Zechariah 14:9). The Gentiles will also be citizens of Christ's worldwide kingdom. Micah 4:2 indicates that they will worship the same Lord: "And many nations shall come, and say, Come, and let us go up to the mountain of the Lord, and to the house of the God of Jacob; and he will teach us of his ways, and we will walk in his paths: for the law shall go forth of Zion, and the word of the Lord from Jerusalem."

God's law for His chosen people will be the law of the Gentiles as well. Gentiles and Jews will be united in their service to Christ. They will serve Him together as brothers, bound with spiritual ties. Isaiah 19:23-25 says that the roadblocks symptomatic of racial division and nationalism will be gone:

> In that day shall there be a highway out of Egypt to Assyria, and the Assyrian shall come into Egypt, and the Egyptian into Assyria, and the Egyptians shall serve with the Assyrians. In that day shall Israel be the third with Egypt and with Assyria, even a blessing in the midst of the land: Whom the Lord of hosts shall bless, saying, Blessed be Egypt my people, and Assyria the work of my hands, and Israel mine inheritance.

What a beautiful day that will be!

The nature of the kingdom will be spiritual. Although material and tangible, the kingdom will essentially be directed by the Spirit of God. For such a thing to be possible on earth, there must be worldwide spiritual cleansing and regeneration. Listen to Ezekiel 36:26-27: "A new heart also will I give you, and a new spirit will I put within you: and I will take away the stony heart out of your flesh, and I will give you an heart of flesh. And I will put my spirit within you, and cause you to walk in my statutes, and ye shall keep my judgments, and do them."

Wars and petty jealousies will be overcome. Social relationships will be healed, and peace will reign. There will no longer be a need for the United Nations. The dream of a perfect society—so elusive in this age—will be a reality in the Millennium under Christ's rule.

There will be physical changes as well. Christ the Great Physician will bring healing, and there will be a restoration of long life. Isaiah 65:20 says, "There shall be no more thence an infant of days, nor an old man that hath not filled his days: for the child shall die an hundred years old; but the sinner being an hundred years old shall be accursed." A hundred years will be such a comparatively short time to live that persons of that age will be considered virtual children. Everyone will live to a full age except those who are accursed and punished with death because of their sin.

Even nature will pass through incredible changes. The earth itself will undergo geological changes, and a new climate will surround mankind. The animal world, which now suffers under the curse brought about by the sin of fallen man, will also experience change. "The wolf and the lamb shall feed together, and the lion shall eat straw like the bullock" (Isaiah 65:25). The problem of a population explosion coupled with food shortages will not exist. The earth will be fruitful and support all mankind.

But the greatest blessing for humanity will be from the spiritual cleansing that comes from Christ. A central sanctuary will be built in Jerusalem from which the Shekinah glory will touch the world. What a glorious world that will be!

10

Retribution

The Judgment That Will Come

Sometimes those of us who hold that the Lord Jesus Christ is coming again are spoken of as pessimists. I think it can be truly said that we are really the only ones who have any right to be optimistic.

—William Culbertson

One of the greatest paintings of all time is Michelangelo's *The Last Judgment.* The action of the painting centers on Christ as He raises His arm in a gesture of damnation. Though some elements of the painting appear unbiblical, at that time its message reminded people of God's holy presence, which had been forgotten in the humanism of the day.

The painting pictures the dead as they are resurrected to be judged. As hell releases its captives, the Judge of Heaven reviews their works. The entire painting reflects the despair of that generation.

When the painting was unveiled, a storm of conviction fell upon the viewers. All Europe trembled as the story of the power of *The Last Judgment* traveled from city to city.

Judgment day comes for everyone. For the athlete it may be the Olympic trials; for the musician it may be an audition or a major performance. For a college student it may be finals.

Accountability and judgment play an important role in every aspect of life. On the job, the employee's work is evaluated. In the government, elected officials are responsible to their constituents. Rewards and penalties are administered on the basis of judgments made every day.

Spiritually, everyone faces ultimate judgment—believers and unbelievers alike. As we saw in chapter 5, the Bible says a day is coming when professing believers will be judged. Works will be revealed, and believers will be judged and rewarded according to what they have done.

Remember, that does not mean salvation can be earned through good works. Scripture is clear that such a thing is impossible. Salvation is by grace through faith (Ephesians 2:8). Judgment, on the other hand, is based on works.

THE NECESSITY OF JUDGMENT

In our society, judgment—as it applies to spiritual matters—is not a popular topic. Most people would prefer to think of God as a loving grandfather figure who does not really care much about sin, as long as the sin is not *too* bad. But the God of the Bible is not like that. He is holy, righteous, pure, and just. He cannot overlook sin, for that would be a violation of His inherent holiness. He cannot ignore sin without making Himself as guilty as the sinner. As Habakkuk said, God is "of purer eyes than to behold evil, and [cannot] look on iniquity" (1:13).

Heaven would not be desirable if God were not a perfectly just judge. Can you imagine heaven if mass murderers and rapists were allowed to live there with impunity? And what of evil rulers such as Nero, who murdered thousands of Christians, and Hitler, who exterminated 6 million Jews? Or what about the many others who have been guilty of oppression and genocide? Would heaven truly be a paradise if they were there, unrepentant and unpunished for their sin?

We view sin through human eyes. We understand the seriousness of the most grotesque sins, but we often fail to understand that to God's pure eyes every sin is grotesque. It was the simple disobedience of Adam that gave birth to all the sin of mankind. No sin, regardless of how small it may seem to us, can be minimized.

God must judge sin in all its forms if He is to be truly just. He could not categorize any sin as insignificant without compromising His holiness. Scripture tells us, "God is light, and in him is no darkness at all" (1 John 1:5). He cannot sin; He cannot overlook sin; and He cannot permit His purity to be sullied by sin of any kind.

THE REALITY OF ACCOUNTABILITY

Many people prefer to live their lives as if they were not accountable to anyone for their beliefs or actions. But that is an unrealistic view of life. In every dimension of life there is accountability. Without it, authority and responsibility would be meaningless.

So it is in the spiritual realm. All of us are accountable to God for how we live, how we obey His Word, how we treat others, how we behave ourselves, and most of all, how we respond to Him. And a day is coming when we will stand before God to give account.

Those who believe in Jesus Christ and have been redeemed understand that accountability. The Holy Spirit is continuously at work in the hearts of believers, exposing sin, convicting, teaching, and guiding. They understand that they are stewards of God's gifts, accountable to Him for how they use them.

But a day is coming when even those who deny God's existence will bow to Him and give account. Those who have neglected Him will have to face Him. Those who have rebelled will stand before Him in judgment. Each one who has rejected God's grace in this life will one day account for his works.

This great, final judgment is known in Scripture as the great white throne judgment. John described it in Revelation 20:11-15:

> And I saw a great white throne, and him that sat on it, from whose face the earth and the heaven fled away; and there was found no place for them. And I saw the dead, small and great, stand before God; and the books were opened: and another book was opened, which is the book of life: and the dead were judged out of those things which were written in the books, according to their works. And the sea gave up the dead which were in it; and death and hell delivered up the dead which

were in them: and they were judged every man according to their works. And death and hell were cast into the lake of fire. This is the second death. And whosoever was not found written in the book of life was cast into the lake of fire.

What makes that awesome scene so fearful is that *all* who stand before the throne that day will be cast into the lake of fire. Not a single name will be found written in the Lamb's book of life, for all the righteous dead will have been judged already at the judgment seat of Christ.

Scripture refers to the lake of fire as "the second death." Those who have not been born again must die again. The second death is not a termination of existence, but eternal separation from the love and grace of God. Revelation 20:10 says that the Beast (Antichrist) and the false prophet will be confined there and tormented day and night forever.

The second death is not some kind of divine torture perpetrated by God. He takes no delight in the death of the wicked. Rather, the torment there is self-inflicted by those who have cut themselves off from God's grace through sin, rebellion, or neglect.

THE IDENTITY OF THE JUDGE

Who is the judge in this ultimate confrontation between God and those who have turned away from Him? It is Jesus Christ Himself. He told His disciples, "For the Father judgeth no man, but hath committed all judgment unto the Son: That all men should honor the Son . . . And hath given him authority to execute judgment also, because he is the Son of man" (John 5:22-23, 27). Peter, speaking of Jesus, said, "He . . . was ordained of God to be the Judge of quick and dead" (Acts 10:42). And Paul taught the same thing: "God . . . commandeth all men every where to repent: Because he hath appointed a day, in the which he will judge the world in righteousness *by that man whom he hath ordained;* whereof he hath given assurance unto all men, in that he hath raised him from the dead" (Acts 17:30-31, italics added).

God gives Jesus Christ authority to judge all men *because of who He is.* Jesus is uniquely qualified to judge because He is God and has existed from eternity (John 1:1). As God, He knows everything, can be everywhere at once, and has unlimited power and authority. He knows everything we think and sees everything we do. Thus He can judge perfectly, with wisdom and full understanding and without error or partiality.

But He is also man. In His incarnation, He left behind the divine privilege that was His as God and became a man. As a man, He humbled Himself and became a servant (Philippians 2:5-8). He knows from experience the temptations we face as human beings. He has been where we are, and He has perfect knowledge of all we go through. Thus He can judge us not only as a sovereign, but as a fellowman. Unlike us, however, Jesus Christ is without sin. He faced every temptation and withstood them all. Thus He can judge righteously, without hypocrisy or guile.

Christ is also uniquely qualified to judge *because of what He has done.* By dying for our sins on the cross, He demonstrated perfect love for all men. Thus, when He judges, His perfect righteousness is balanced by His perfect love.

When Jesus Christ died on the cross for our sins, He was bearing the wrath of God on our behalf. Because He was without sin and therefore guiltless, He did not deserve to die. But He accepted death on our behalf, thereby making forgiveness possible for us.

Righteousness demands that sin be punished. As we have seen, God cannot simply overlook sin and offer forgiveness without penalty. But since the penalty for sin is death, God Himself in the form of Jesus Christ paid the penalty for us. Because of His sacrifice, He can offer forgiveness to those who yield to Him in faith.

Those who reject Christ's work on their behalf will be judged. Because Christ took the judgment for our sins upon Himself, He has been given authority by the Father to execute judgment on those who reject His grace.

THE FINALITY OF THE JUDGMENT

Christ humbled Himself for our sake, and because of His sacrifice God has elevated Him to the supreme position of judge over all. Philippians 2:10-11 says, "That at the name of Jesus every knee should bow, of things in heaven, and things in earth, and things under the earth; and that every tongue should confess that Jesus Christ is Lord, to the glory of God the Father."

The choice is not *whether* we will bow to Jesus Christ as

Lord, but *when*. If we confess Him as Savior now, we will not face Him as judge at the great white throne. Scripture proclaims, "Now is the accepted time; behold, now is the day of salvation" (2 Corinthians 6:2).

By the time of the great white throne judgment, everyone's choice will already have been made. Many people will be there who simply postponed or neglected choosing, but it will be too late for them to make a decision then. Only the accounting for works done in the flesh will be left, and then the awful, final, and irreversible judgment.

If you are a Christian, you do not need to fear facing Christ in judgment at the great white throne. He has already borne your judgment Himself. But perhaps you have relatives and friends who are without Christ. Do you sense the importance of praying for them, witnessing to them, and living as a good testimony? They are facing judgment and eternity separated from Jesus Christ.

If you are not a Christian, please open your life to Christ today. Although you exist in time, you must plan for eternity. Now that you have been exposed to the truth and have the opportunity, it is time to decide. Those who delay find their souls become hardened to the truth of Scripture and the promptings of the Spirit of God.

"To day if ye will hear his voice, harden not your hearts" (Hebrews 3:15).

11

Realization

Beyond All Time

The latter truth [the second coming of Christ] transformed my whole idea of life; it broke the power of the world and its ambition over me, and filled my life with the most radiant optimism even under the most discouraging circumstances.
—R. A. Torrey

Puritan writer Thomas Watson said, "Eternity to the godly is a day that has no sunset; eternity to the wicked is a night that has no sunrise." Eternity is the grand climax of all history. It is the age to come when every person will acknowledge Jesus as Lord. Eternity will bring to this world all God intended for us. Sin will have been judged and banished. Rewards will have been presented. Life will continue with new vitality, meaning, and perfection. What an age that will be!

The dictionary defines eternity as "the quality or fact of being eternal; without beginning or end; timeless." It is the endless time after death—future life and immortality. It is a time beyond all time.

The prospect of eternity is exciting and mind-boggling, and it is especially intriguing for believers in Jesus Christ. In this life there are many broken hearts, but in eternity there will be unending satisfaction and fullness of joy. Here we face sickness, sin, and separation; in eternity we will know none of those things. The psalmist writes, "Thou wilt shew me the path of life: in thy presence is fulness of joy; at thy right hand there are pleasures *for evermore*" (Psalm 16:11, italics added). God has planned eternity especially for the pleasure of His children—those who have trusted Jesus Christ and have been born again.

The nineteenth-century American preacher William Jackson once said, "Here on earth our greatest joys are empty and imperfect. But in the presence of God, we shall have fullness of joy. Our cup of joy will be full. There will be no room for sorrow. Here our sweetest pleasures are but momentary. They fly away, and are replaced by bitter disappointment. But at God's right hand, there are 'pleasures forevermore.' "

What is eternity like? Does the Bible give us enough information to prepare us for eternity? While the information the Bible gives is limited, it is certainly sufficient to guide us in our understanding.

ALL CREATION WILL BE DIFFERENT

Life here on earth makes eternity appealing. Here we live in the midst of pain, hunger, sickness, sorrow, war, disaster, and loss. Eternity will be free from all those effects of the curse.

In the beginning God's creation was perfect and complete, free from the threat of death and deterioration. But all of nature was marred by one man's sin. The curse that resulted from Adam's sin affected the earth, the animals, and everything that man could touch.

Romans 8:22 acknowledges that, saying, "For we know that the whole creation groaneth and travaileth in pain together until now." Every element of nature is somehow affected by man's sin. But in eternity, all of nature will be redeemed from the effects of the curse and restored to perfection as God originally planned.

God will make a new creation. The apostle John describes this change in Revelation 21:1: "And I saw a new heaven and a new earth: for the first heaven and the first earth were passed away." Revelation 20:11 also speaks of the passing away of the old. At the great white throne—the place of judgment for those who are indifferent and unbelieving—"the earth and the heaven fled away." The new creation takes place after the judgment of the unrighteous. The unrighteous are first banished to the lake of fire where their sin cannot corrupt the new universe.

Bible scholar Herman Hoyt believes the idea of the words *fled away* or *passed away* refers to a "rearrangement of order." He writes: "By means of the flood, a previous order passed away. . . . The present heavens and earth are to undergo a similar change by means of fire . . . [This will bring about] the removal of all evidence of evil works."[1]

Peter also describes these changes in his second epistle: "But the day of the Lord will come as a thief in the night; in which the heavens shall pass away with a great noise, and the elements shall melt with fervent heat, the earth also and the works that are therein shall be burned up" (2 Peter 3:10).

THE ENVIRONMENT WILL BE PERFECT

The new earth will be a perfect earth in which to live and serve. It will be a world where the righteous will serve God unhindered by selfishness or the evil desires of the flesh.

In our world the righteous are out of place. According to Hebrews 11:13, they are "strangers and pilgrims on the earth." They live a different life and walk a different walk. They have different goals. They have godly desires and interests in the midst of a world system that is totally given over to ungodliness. Much of what is printed, televised, and sold is aimed at the ungodly of the world. But in eternity, things will be new.

The apostle Peter was present that night in the upper room when Jesus gave this blessed promise: "I go to prepare a place for you. And if I go and prepare a place for you, I will come again, and receive you unto myself; that where I am, there you may be also" (John 14:2-3). How Peter must have looked forward to the time when he would once again walk and live with the Lord Jesus—except this time in a perfect environment, prepared especially by Jesus Himself.

1. Herman A. Hoyt, *The End Times* (Chicago: Moody, 1969), p. 224.

Peter wrote, "We . . . look for new heavens and a new earth, wherein dwelleth righteousness" (2 Peter 3:13). He viewed that breath-taking prospect as a motivation to be diligent in the pursuit of holiness in this age. He added, "Seeing that ye look for such things, be diligent that ye may be found of him in peace, without spot, and blameless" (v. 14). Peter is saying, "In light of eternity, live right."

THE HOLY CITY WILL BE THE HUB

In addition to the universal changes that will come about in eternity, there will be organizational changes. The city of the living God—the New Jerusalem—will transcend heaven to be a part of the new earth. It will be the centerpiece and hub of the eternal realm, uniting heaven and earth. John said, "And I . . . saw the holy city, new Jerusalem, coming down from God out of heaven, prepared as a bride adorned for her husband" (Revelation 21:2).

Old Testament saints longed for that city whose builder and maker is God. Abraham, Isaac, and Jacob anticipated it: "They desire[d] a better country, that is, an heavenly: wherefore God is not ashamed to be called their God: for he hath prepared for them a city" (Hebrews 11:16).

This eternal city will be the home of God the Father, God the Son, and God the Holy Spirit. Its citizens will include all the righteous of God's creation from all ages. Angels will be there. The church will be there. Both Old Testament saints and Tribulation saints will call it home. It will be a beautiful, glorious place, and righteousness will prevail forever.

WE WILL BE CHANGED

Not only will there be universal and organizational changes in eternity, but things will also be different for those who have put their faith in Jesus Christ. The curse imposed because of sin will be gone. The sin that threw the world into disorder will be removed. The earth will be transformed into the beautiful place it was meant to be in the Garden of Eden.

The bodies of the redeemed of eternity will be glorified. And finally, we will be all that God wants us to be. Here on earth now, we are often disappointed because instead of being like Him, we are faded, frail imitations. But in eternity, we *will* be like Him. Hebrews 12:22-23 says, "But ye are come unto mount Sion, and unto the city of the living God, the heavenly Jerusalem, and to an innumerable company of angels, to the general assembly and church of the firstborn, which are written in heaven, and to God the Judge of all, and to the spirits of *just men made perfect*" (italics added). The former evil nature of those in the city of the living God is gone. Sin has passed away. Having seen Jesus Christ with unveiled eyes, they have become like Him (1 John 3:2).

Everyone in heaven will be wholly sanctified. Sanctification is a continuing work here on earth, but in eternity the process will be complete. No sinful thing will ever enter that eternal world. Revelation 21:27 says, "And there shall in no wise enter into it any thing that defileth, neither whatsoever worketh abomination, or maketh a lie: but they which are written in the Lamb's book of life."

The New Jerusalem will be a holy city (Revelation 21:10), with holy people, unlike anything we here on earth can imagine. The people of that city will be free of pain and death: "And God shall wipe away all tears from their eyes; and there shall be no more death, neither sorrow, nor crying, neither shall there be any more pain: for the former things are passed away" (Revelation 21:4).

Believers will finally inherit all things. They will realize the consummation of the promise that they would be joint heirs with Christ. Peter said of this inheritance that it is "incorruptible, and undefiled, and [one] that fadeth not away, reserved in heaven for you" (1 Peter 1:4).

GOD'S PERFECT WILL WILL BE DONE

In eternity, the church will sit with the King on His throne as the Bride of Christ. Believers will have the place of highest honor as they rule together with Christ. Although Scripture does not spell out specific responsibilities, believers will have positions of authority. Revelation 2:26 says, "He that overcometh, and keepeth my works unto the end, to him will I give power over the nations." The church will rule with Christ, playing an essential role in seeing that God's will is done "in earth, as it is in heaven" (Matthew 6:10).

The saints of the Old Testament and the Tribulation saints will be given places of responsibility as well. They will be seen as friends and attendants to Christ and His Bride and will also share responsibility with Christ in His rulership over the new heaven and new earth.

In eternity all the promises of God for His children will be fulfilled. There will be no strife between nations, for all men will want God's will. All of creation and redeemed mankind will continue as God meant them to be, perfect in unity and working together for the glory of God.

> One short life for watching with the Saviour,
> Eternal years to walk with Him in white,
> One short life to bravely meet disaster,
> Eternal years to reign with Him in light,
> One brief life for weary toils and trials,
> Eternal years for calm and peaceful rest,
> One brief life for patient self-denials,
> Eternal years for life, where life is best.
>
> (Author unknown)

Have you considered the prospect of eternity? Have you considered your relationship to Jesus Christ? That is what will determine how and where you will spend the ages to come. While Scripture teaches how satisfying life is in God's eternal city, it also teaches that eternal judgment awaits those who are spiritually indifferent. Hebrews 2:3 asks, "How shall we escape, if we neglect so great salvation?" It is not necessary to reject God's salvation and sovereignty: neglect alone will condemn a man.

The five foolish virgins in Matthew 25 were not against God or the bridegroom. They were simply neglectful and unprepared. They failed to get oil, and therefore they were shut out from the marriage feast. Neglect alone can block your entrance into eternity with the redeemed of God. Are you prepared for eternity? Christ has made heaven a prepared place for a prepared people. At His right hand "there are pleasures for evermore" (Psalm 16:11).

12

Reassurance

Jesus' Last Message

The world is full of experiments for bringing deliverance to the race, but on the authority of the New Testament and in the light of nineteen centuries of history, I declare my conviction that the only hope of this world is the return of Christ to reign over the earth and to establish universal peace.

—A. J. Gordon

The study of prophecy offers hope to the believer. It also gives a sense of urgency to the task of evangelism. The more we see Bible prophecies heading toward fulfillment in contemporary world events, the more we are struck with the sense that there is not much time left to reach the lost with the message of God's saving grace. It is a sobering thought. The prophetic passages of Scripture are filled with fervent invitations to turn to the Lord. I continue to be amazed at the number of people I meet who have come to Christ through the study of Bible prophecy.

I believe every time Jesus Christ opened His mouth to speak of future events, His heart was filled with anguish for those who were headed for a Christless eternity. When He spoke of future things, there was an urgent plea—either implied or directly expressed in His words—imploring those who had not committed their lives to God in faith to surrender to Him at that moment.

The study of prophecy is fruitless for those whose only concern is curiosity about the future. It is not merely an academic subject to be digested, categorized, and filed away for later reference. Bible prophecy is full of practical truth and life-changing revelation. The message of the prophetic passages of Scripture is that *life is serious business, and the pursuit of God's glory is central to every other issue.*

If we study prophecy and miss that truth, the study is in vain. Yet I fear that in all that has been written and spoken about Bible prophecy in the past few years, this essential truth has somehow become obscured. Yet that does not diminish the importance of understanding what God says about the future.

It is significant to note that the final message of Jesus Christ in Scripture—Revelation 22:7-21—is an application of the truth of the prophecy contained in the book of Revelation. There Christ reiterates the promise of His return, gives some final exhortations, and closes with an invitation to unbelievers. Three times in that chapter He says, "Behold, I come quickly," and each time He makes that promise it is accompanied by an exhortation.

I AM COMING: KEEP MY WORD!

His first exhortation is to revere God's Word. "Behold, I come quickly: blessed is he that keepeth the sayings of the prophecy of this book" (Revelation 22:7). This is a recurring theme throughout the book of Revelation. In chapter 1, John wrote, "Blessed is he that readeth, and they that hear the words of this prophecy, and *keep* those things which are written therein: for the time is at hand" (v. 3, italics added). The obvious message is that in light of the Lord's imminent return, the number one priority is the *Word of God.*

We tend to get caught up easily in the cares of this world: money, business, future plans, as well as other things that consume our attention. In their proper place, those things are not wrong. But they are not the priorities.

The only thing that truly counts is the glory of God, and the expectation of Jesus' return has a way of putting that into perspective. Jesus said, "Seek ye first the kingdom of God, and his righteousness; and all these things shall be added unto you" (Matthew 6:33). Somehow, knowing that the Kingdom age may come soon helps us focus on seeking God's righteousness.

Over the years, I have noticed that the Christians who seem to have the highest regard for God's Word tend to be those who are most consciously looking for the Lord's return. They know the brevity of this life, and they are planning for eternity. Consequently, their values are eternal values, and the Word of God is a high priority.

I AM COMING: OBEY MY WORD!

Jesus' second exhortation in Revelation 22 is a call for obedience. "And, behold, I come quickly; and my reward is with me, to give every man according as his work shall be. I am Alpha and Omega, the beginning and the end, the first and the last. Blessed are they that do his commandments" (vv. 12-14).

If knowing the Lord may return at any time does not move you to greater obedience, then you have not responded in faith to the promise of His return. Nothing stirs the heart of a true believer more than the expectation that his Lord may appear at any instant.

Remember the parable of the talents in Matthew 25? A man went into a far country, leaving his servants in charge of his money with the promise that he would return. The servants who believed him were obedient and invested the money wisely. However, the servant who was careless and unbelieving buried his money, not expecting his master's promised return to occur so suddenly. When the master did return, the disobedient servant was ashamed. His unbelief had led to carelessness and ultimately to disobedience.

Living with the expectation of Jesus' return is a dynamic motivation to obedience. Knowing that we could be face-to-face with Jesus at any moment has a way of keeping our affections and desires in line with His will. We want to obey so that we will not be ashamed at His coming.

I AM COMING: SPREAD MY WORD!

Jesus' final exhortation—the last word from our Lord in the Bible—is an invitation to come to Him for salvation and an admonition to believers to join in the task of evangelism.

"And the Spirit and the bride say, Come. And let him that heareth say, Come. And let him that is athirst come. And whosoever will, let him take the water of life freely" (Revelation 22:17).

It has been estimated that the word *come* appears over six hundred times in the Bible. Someone has expressed its inclusiveness in this way:

> C represents the children,
> O represents the old people,
> M represents the middle-aged, and
> E is for everybody!

At least it is pleasant to think of the word *come* in that way. God is so interested in our relationship to Him that Scripture concludes with an invitation: "The Spirit and the bride say, Come" (Revelation 22:17). The Holy Spirit invites us to come. The *bride* probably refers to the church, composed of all believers in Jesus Christ; and in light of Christ's return they are encouraged to spread the Word.

The invitation is *costly*. Behind every invitation there is a price to be paid. The price of this invitation was the sacrificial death of Christ for our sins (Mark 15:22-34). The invitation is also *timely:* "And let him that is athirst come" (Revelation 22:17). Every person has a basic thirst that can only be satisfied by Jesus Christ. The French mathematician and philosopher Blaise Pascal is credited with describing this need as a God-shaped vacuum in every heart. Jesus Christ has already provided the way to fulfillment. He promises, "Whosoever drinketh of the water that I shall give him shall *never thirst*" (John 4:14, italics added).

The Scottish poet Robert Burns recognized the center of fulfillment in his "Epistle to Davie, a Brother Poet":

> It's no in titles nor in rank,
> It's no in wealth like Lon'on Bank,
> To purchase peace and rest.
> It's no in makin muckle, mair;
> It's no in books, it's no in lear,
> To make us truly blest;
> If happiness have not her seat
> An' centre in the breast. . . .

Last, the invitation is *inclusive*. "And whosoever will, let him take the water of life freely" (Revelation 22:17). In light of the imminent return of Christ, believers are to spread the gospel, sharing God's Word because of the knowledge we have. *To know is to owe!* Our blessings make us responsible. *To have is to owe!* Our mission is clearly defined: "Go ye therefore, and teach all nations, baptizing them in the name of the Father, and of the Son, and of the Holy Ghost: Teaching them to observe all things whatsoever I have commanded you: and lo, I am with you alway, even unto the end of the world" (Matthew 28:19-20).

The story is told of a silver shortage for making currency during the reign of Oliver Cromwell. Representatives carefully searched the empire to find the scarce metal. After months of investigation, the committee reported that they had found no silver except in the cathedrals where the images of saints were made of silver. To this Oliver Cromwell is said to have eloquently suggested that they melt down the saints and put them into circulation.

That is the need of the church in light of the coming of Christ. The invitation is open. The hour is late. The time is at hand. "He which testifieth these things saith, Surely I come quickly. Amen. Even so, come, Lord Jesus" (Revelation 22:20).